CHICKEN SOUP
FOR THE
BREAST CANCER
SURVIVOR'S SOUL

Chicken Soup for the Breast Cancer Survivor's Soul
Stories to Inspire, Support and Heal
Jack Canfield, Mark Victor Hansen, Mary Olsen Kelly

Published by Backlist, LLC,
a unit of Chicken Soup for the Soul Publishing, LLC. www.chickensoup.com

Front cover book design Andrea Perrine Brower
Originally published in 2006 by Health Communications, Inc.

Back cover and spine redesign by Pneuma Books, LLC

Distributed to the booktrade by Simon & Schuster. SAN: 200-2442

Publisher's Cataloging-in-Publication Data
(Prepared by The Donohue Group)

Chicken soup for the breast cancer survivor's soul : stories to inspire, support and heal / [compiled by] Jack Canfield, Mark Victor Hansen, [and]
Mary Olsen Kelly.

   p. : ill. ; cm.

   Originally published: Deerfield Beach, FL : Health Communications, c2006.
   ISBN: 978-1-62361-049-4

   1. Breast--Cancer--Popular works. 2. Breast--Cancer--Anecdotes. 3.
Anecdotes. I. Canfield, Jack, 1944- II. Hansen, Mark Victor. III. Kelly, Mary
Olsen.

RC280.B8 C352 2012
616.99/4/49   2012944293

PRINTED IN THE UNITED STATES OF AMERICA
on acid free paper
23 22 21 20 19 18   06 07 08 09 10 11

CHICKEN SOUP
FOR THE
BREAST CANCER
SURVIVOR'S SOUL

Stories to Inspire, Support and Heal

Jack Canfield
Mark Victor Hansen
Mary Olsen Kelly

Backlist, LLC, a unit of
Chicken Soup for the Soul Publishing, LLC
Cos Cob, CT
www.chickensoup.com

"This is nothing compared to that sinking feeling I got when they told me I have breast cancer."

Contents

3. CHALLENGES

4. CHARACTER

Introduction

Going through the experience of breast cancer is no picnic, but with loving support, helpful advice and the healing power of laughter, it can be achieved. It is our fondest hope that you will be encouraged, buoyed, uplifted and instructed by the stories contained in this book. Other breast-cancer survivors wrote them for you— to bring you hope, to give you strength and courage.

Research has shown that those who attend support groups tend to have higher survival rates. Those who reach out to family and friends for love and support make it through the medical journey of breast cancer more successfully. We have so much to learn from each other as we face the challenges of healing ourselves; often someone who has gone through the journey before us shares the thing we need to learn.

We all have a story to tell. Our stories are healing and have power. We encourage you to tell your story, too. Who knows? Your story might encourage someone to go for a mammogram, even save someone's life.

Melissa Etheridge talks about how she prepared for the journey of breast cancer by gathering her "flashlights"— her friends and family members who would help her shine light into the fearful darkness.

This collection of stories can be one of those flashlights for you—shining light and making your way easier, helping you to feel stronger, more filled with love and encouraged by the knowledge that you're not alone in your journey.

1
LOVE

Who so loves believes the impossible.

Elizabeth Barrett Browning

She's My Hero

Things do not change; we change.

Henry David Thoreau

Senior year in high school: a time of college choices, graduations, proms and carefree friendships. Most kids were busy soaking up the last drop of the irresponsibility of high school before having to grow up in college. Most kids were making last-minute memories and losing them just as quickly. Most kids were having the time of their lives. Most kids didn't have a mother diagnosed with breast cancer. I wasn't like most kids.

I was on my way to a soccer team dinner with my friend, Bill. I opened the front door and saw my parents sitting at the kitchen table with their heads down. My mother turned to me with a tear-soaked face, and before I could ask what was wrong, she answered me.

"I have breast cancer."

"Are you going to be all right?"

"I hope so."

Confused, I walked down the hall into my bedroom. I

looked at the walls covered with my favorite sports heroes and stared at each poster, looking for answers to the questions swimming in my head. *What does she mean she has breast cancer? It was probably just a mistake, right? No one actually dies from that, right? Right?*

I returned to the kitchen without the words to respond to what was going on, what I was feeling. I didn't know what I was feeling.

"Can I go to the team dinner?" I asked.

"Of course, sweetheart," my mother replied.

I climbed back into the car with Bill, who noticed I was shaken. He asked me, "What's wrong?"

"My mother just told me she has breast cancer."

He asked if I wanted to stay, and I told him I didn't. I wanted to go away and come back later—when we could start this all over and my mother wouldn't be ill. She wasn't even fifty years old.

During my mother's bout with breast cancer, finding out she had the disease has remained the clearest scene in my mind. The following months I watched everything blur as she received a litany of radiation and chemotherapy treatments. She would struggle out of bed each day, burned from the radiation, only to get sick in the bathroom. Her hair began falling out, bags permanently hung under her eyes, and the color vanished from her face. This woman was looking less and less like my mother each day.

Then I looked at the picture of me with my parents taken in much happier times. We were all smiling without a care in the world, and I would have done anything to stay locked in that moment forever. I'd look at my father in the photo and then to me, thinking another possibility: *The next picture may just be the two of us.* Tears welled up in my eyes as I thought about what it would be like going to college later that year without my mother to call. Things would get blurry all over again.

One night as I looked at that picture, I focused on my mother's face. She hadn't smiled like that in a long time. Her hair was long and thick, and her face was youthful and beaming, but it was her eyes I noticed the most. They illuminated the whole picture with their vibrancy and life. If eyes really are windows to the soul, then this woman's soul was bright enough to light up the rest of us.

"Are you doing all right, sweetheart?" I heard from behind. I spun around to see my mother walking up to me in her robe. Her head was almost bald, her face was tired and worn, and her shoulders hung limp. But suddenly I felt in my heart that everything would be all right because when I saw her eyes, they were the same eyes that lit up that family picture. I saw that same bright soul shining through like the sun behind a set of gray clouds. I didn't say anything, but my mother could read what I was thinking. She just grabbed my hands and told me, "We're going to get through this."

From that day on, I've thought of my mother as nothing short of an angel. This woman conquered a disease inside her, one that was ripping away many of her physical attributes. It took away her hair; it took away her appetite; it took away her energy; it even took away her smile. But it never took away her soul, her spirit, for that remained where it belonged—with her family—and it was never cancer's to take.

I realized then that while she drew her spirit and strength from my father and me, we did the same from her. It's ironic to think that I would not have made it through my mother's battle with cancer without my mother's support, but that was certainly the case. Our family unit laughed more, shared more, loved more. We knew the only way we were going to beat this thing was to love each other more and more every day.

Cancer can't touch love if it's not allowed to. It will try

to trick you into thinking that it can take away everything. It's like that set of gray clouds. It can cover the sun and make you think everything is dreary, somber and hopeless. It tends to make things blurry. But if you have faith, patience, courage and love, eventually those clouds have to move, and the sun that was hidden will smile warmly on you once again.

Now I think back upon that day when I walked into my bedroom for answers. I looked at Michael Jordan, Don Mattingly and Patrick Ewing, men I'd anointed as my heroes, for some guidance. All my life I had followed these men as people I'd like to be like one day. But all they did was play a sport. They didn't fight for their lives with their backs against the wall. They hadn't had to look cancer straight in the face and say, "No!" I had spent my whole life looking outside for a hero when I should have been looking within.

It's been nearly ten years since my mother was diagnosed with breast cancer, and she is totally healthy now. I have certainly endured some tough times since my senior year in high school, but I have faced those situations with a new perspective. I watched my mother prevail in the toughest fight of all, and I know deep in my heart that I have some of that magic myself because she's given it to me. However, I take solace in knowing that whenever I may lose my way or things get blurry again, my mother will always be there to tell me: "We're going to get through this."

She is, and always will be, my hero.

Anthony Burton

Night School

Cancer got me over unimportant fears, like getting old.

Olivia Newton-John

Without a doubt, the nights were the worst.

During the daytime, family and friends visited and chatted. Others called to talk on the phone. My mother rented movies, and we watched them together. My teenage sons went through the typical trials and tribulations of that phase of life, and its inherent daily drama kept my thoughts occupied. Visits to the oncology clinic or the radiation therapy center at the hospital provided opportunities to visit with other patients and cheerful nurses and technicians. And the daylight somehow made everything okay. It was easier to laugh in the daytime, and it was easier to believe I would get well. I didn't feel so alone when the sun was up.

But when night fell, everything changed. The nightmares of childhood could not compete with the horrors of those nights when survival seemed only a very slim possibility. With everyone in our household sound asleep and not a sound to be heard anywhere, I would bolt upright in my bed, heart pounding, envisioning things I feared would come to pass. I would start to tremble all over, pull the blankets tighter around me, and lie there shivering and sobbing for what seemed like hours.

Then I heard someone refer to those times as "God's night classes." She said that God often awakens us in the middle of the night during difficult times for the simple reason that it is quiet and there is nothing to distract us from communicating with him. With all around us dark and silent, we can talk to him, and we can listen to what he has to tell us.

I began to look at those nightly wake-up calls as God's night classes. When I began to shake all over and the tears came, I begged him to pull me close, to comfort me and calm my fears. I told him where it hurt and what I was afraid of. And, yes, I prayed for a cure. But mostly I just prayed for courage to get through one more treatment, one more surgery, one more day of living with cancer.

After a few of these "night classes," the trembling and the tears stopped. If I awoke during the night, I said, "Hello, God. I'm here."

Invariably he said, "So am I."

Kathy Cawthon

Sooner or Later

You don't get to choose how you're going to die. Or when. You can only decide how you're going to live. Now.

Joan Baez

On April 15, 1997, I was diagnosed with inflammatory breast cancer. Talk about an emotional roller-coaster: I felt shock and fear, denial and fear, anger and fear . . . a lot of fear.

The only thing that got me through that crazy earth-quake of a time was that so many people offered so much help. Every day I got phone calls, e-mails, cards, letters, books, tapes, meals . . . you name it. There were on-line support groups, face-to-face support groups, dance move-ment therapy classes, art therapy classes, healing circles. There were friends, relatives, neighbors, therapists, social workers, ministers. I literally owe my life to all those peo-ple. But the person who helped me the most during that terrible time was my son John, six years old.

Because the perspective of a six-year-old is so different from an adult, I had to think in a very different way in order to help him understand what was happening. Little did I know at the time how much John would help me break through my fear barrier.

The first step in my treatment plan was chemotherapy. I felt a lot of fear about having chemo. I thought of it as poison and wondered if it would do more harm than good, but I certainly couldn't describe it that way to John. I told him that, since I had a powerful sickness in my body, I would need powerful medicine to help me get better. The medicine was so powerful, in fact, that it was superhero medicine—it could knock the hair right off my head!

John was obsessed with Batman, Superman and the Power Rangers. He loved the thought that his mom's life was being saved by medicine that was as strong as his heroes, and so he was thrilled when my hair was "knocked right off my head." I found myself visualizing little Supermans flying through my body punching out all the cancer cells, and I wasn't scared anymore.

Once four months' worth of chemo was done, I moved on to the next step of my treatment: surgery.

I have never been particularly breast-identified, but a body part is a body part, and my goal has always been to retain as many of mine as possible. I dreaded the prospect of losing my breast. John was horrified.

Over the next few days, my six-year-old son worked feverishly, concocting alternate ways for the doctor to get the cancer out of my body without having to cut off my breast. His favorite, and most creative, idea was for the doctor to go into my body through my mouth and use a spoon to scoop out the sick parts of my breast from the inside, without having to touch the outside at all.

In discussing each of his proposals, together John and I realized and came to accept that losing a breast might just be the best way to help me get better. Suddenly, I was no longer afraid of the impending surgery.

But it was toward the end of my treatment that my son helped me the most.

One day, shortly before I started radiation, we were sitting in the living room. I think I was watching him play with Legos. Out of the blue (which is how kids ambush you with the big stuff), he said, "Mommy, if they don't get the sickness out of your body in time, will you die?"

Well, I did not want to go there, so I said something like, "John, you know that eventually everything dies."

He looked at me as if I were a total idiot and replied, "I know that, Mommy. What *I* mean is, if they don't get the sickness out of your body in time, will you die *sooner*?"

Then it hit me: It wasn't about whether I died sooner—or later—but that I really lived while I was here.

John's question made me realize that there's more than one way to die. And that day I decided that I didn't want to die before my time—I didn't want to die *sooner*—because I was living in fear. That day, I saw that I might not be able to control whether or not I recovered from breast cancer or its treatment, but I could control how I spent the time I had left, regardless of whether it was long or short.

My son helped me break the cycle of fear in which I had been trapped. His search for understanding led me to my *own* understanding—and that changed my life. You see, whether I die sooner or later, I've got a whole bunch of moments left to live. And I plan on living every one of them—right now.

Lori Misicka

Family

The greatest discovery of my generation is that a human being can alter his life by altering the attitude of his mind.

William James

"Grandpa, do you hurt?"
"Grandpa, do you want something to eat or drink?"
"Do you want a pillow to sit on so you're comfortable?"
"Where does it hurt, Grandpa?"

I have been a male breast-cancer survivor for nine years. Many people don't realize that men can contract it. When I was diagnosed and people found out I had cancer, most assumed it was some other form—lung, liver or skin.

I received support from many people: my wife, children, church family, friends and coworkers. The support of the grandchildren was especially wonderful to observe. All our children live at least one day's drive away, so I didn't see them often until I had begun treatment and lost all my hair. I continued to work throughout my treatment, so I was able to visit our children and grandchildren as I traveled to their cities.

One of our sons and his family did come to visit us after

I had started chemotherapy and was bald. His son, about three, wanted me to play with him. As we played with the small cars and trucks, he would reach over and remove the baseball cap that I wore and rub my bald head, then replace the hat and continue playing. I don't know why, and he didn't say anything, but maybe it was his way of soothing a sick Grandpa.

I also visited our other children and grandchildren on a business trip to their cities. Before I arrived, I called the parents and told them they should probably talk to the children before I got there and tell them I was now bald and why. It happened the same way with each family: When I arrived, we would sit and talk about normal family things, but not sickness. However, the minute that both parents were out of the room, the grandchildren asked considerate questions. If a parent returned, the conversation returned to school, birthdays or Grandma. I think children are the best examples of caring and support. They aren't afraid of asking questions or of being embarrassed by questions that an adult may hesitate to ask.

I think the best way to show concern and support for a cancer patient or survivor is to ask the question that's on your mind and offer help or assistance. It is the responsibility of the survivor to be open and willing to talk about the illness—then others will be more comfortable talking honestly with you.

I received much support from many people during my treatment and recovery, and it meant a lot to my wife and our family to see the concern that people have for each other. I find that many cancer patients don't have anyone to talk to, and they welcome conversation about what they are going through or will soon have to face. Our grandchildren showed me the true sincerity that children have, and we should all model that simplicity when placed in situations of concern for others.

Lowell Gere

You'll Never Feel So Loved

Where there is great love, there are always miracles.

Willa Cather

A few days after hearing the devastating news that the shadow on the mammogram was indeed cancer, I received a call I'll never forget from an aunt who was a breast-cancer survivor. The only part of the conversation I remember was one simple line: "You'll never feel so loved." At the time I had no clue what that could mean, but I thanked her for calling and began the journey that every cancer patient goes through.

I began to understand the power of these five little words a few days after my aunt's call, when I telephoned my daughter about the diagnosis and the upcoming surgery. Her first words were simple and direct: "I'm on my way!" Not, "What can I do?" Or, "I'll try to come," or even "Do you want me to come?" but simply, "I'm on my way!" With the support and encouragement from her husband, my daughter was with me until I no longer needed her help. I felt so loved.

Later that same day, with only twenty minutes' notice, a friend volunteered to meet my husband and me at the doctor's office to be the extra ears and note taker. Quietly, in the background, she was the one who held it together when my husband left the room (sick), and I began crying. She asked all the right questions and later went over the facts one by one, helping us comprehend all that was happening. What a gift! I knew she cared about us, and I felt so loved.

In spite of all the frightening, horrific things that were taking place, I began to understand how the love of God and others would carry me through, and I knew I would be able to conquer this thing called cancer. The love was manifested in so many ways: cards, calls, prayers, meals and sometimes just one little sentence would carry me through a difficult day.

I remember my husband holding me in his arms, reading from a book given to me from a coworker of his, also a breast-cancer survivor, who was sure we would both enjoy reading it. I was too tired, so he read aloud every night, and we laughed and cried together. I not only felt his love, but also was touched by the fact that someone I had never met cared enough to think of me.

I had retired the year before my diagnosis, and one day a former coworker of mine stopped by with a basket full of thoughtful gifts from friends at the office: a warm hat to cover my thinning hair, inspirational books to lift my spirits, aromatherapy candles and bubble bath to soothe my body, and much more. They cared enough to remember me, and I felt so loved!

In times of need, everyone knows that family will be there for you, but I was overwhelmed by the way my immediate and extended family came through. Parents, sisters and in-laws joined together to provide support and encouragement in so many wonderful ways. They were with me every step of the way. In fact, my sister was there when I had my last chemotherapy session, and a niece planned a big surprise party to celebrate the end of my treatments!

A daughter-in-law, without being asked, came and cleaned our whole house; our sons provided hugs, teasing and comforting words; neighbors and friends brought meals. The prayers, flowers, calls and cards of countless others were all given in the name of love. These are the things I still remember today because they carried me through a difficult time, and I am filled with gratitude.

As I look back, I have experienced what my aunt meant when she said, "You'll never feel so loved." In great part because of this love I am a cancer survivor. Yes, the treatments and advice of wonderful doctors and the prayers of many helped save my life, but I also believe that if the soul is being fed, the body will heal.

If you are going through a journey like mine, look for all the love that is being sent your way, for you will be comforted and treasured. Believe me, you'll never feel so loved!

Sharon Bomgaars

Food Is Love

Difficult times have helped me to understand better than before how infinitely rich and beautiful life is.

Isak Dinesen

Gasping for breath, as though a vacuum had suddenly sucked the air from the room, I heard the doctor tell my sister, "Your margins were not clear" from the lumpectomy they had performed earlier that week. The doctor wanted to cut more. "I feel the lymph glands may be involved, and the cancer cells in the lump are a fast-growing variety of breast cancer."

My sister Mary (called Meemee), her husband and I went into the waiting room at the doctor's office to schedule the return surgery. I was fighting to keep back the tears, not wanting to add to the misery already in the room. Sweeping the two of them into a spontaneous group hug, we rocked together in the waiting room while the nurses and staff looked on in sympathy and some embarrassment. My stomach clenched into a completely new and unexpected knot. My perfect sister—the one who was always strong and capable, the one I'd always turned to for my own comfort and support, the one who was never sick or dejected—was suddenly badly hurt. Cancer! Life-threatening, terrifying cancer! Not my sister! Through no fault of her own, she was really sick. My thoughts were jumbled. *What can I do? I have to do something. I have to make her well! She can't be sick, and she certainly can't die! I have to do something.* It became a mantra of sorts—my internal litany: *Do something, do something to heal Meemee!*

So I got to work. Ever since I was allowed in the kitchen as a child, I've shown my love for the people I care about through cooking. My signature cookies, the many meals I've prepared through the years, are the stuff of legend in our family. It's my role in our very close family, and one I don't take lightly. So, faced with the awesome task I'd set myself, I did research into the effects of food on healing, particularly healing from the effects of chemotherapy and radiation on the body. I learned about the cancer-fighting properties in phytochemicals, substances found in fruits and vegetables that work in a variety of ways to build the immune system and destroy carcinogens in our bodies. The ten most phyto-chemical-rich foods known are cruciferous vegetables like broccoli, beans (especially soybeans), berries and cherries, onions and garlic, carotenoid-rich vegetables like carrots and sweet potatoes, fish, tomatoes, mushrooms, all nuts and seeds (especially flax seeds), and green tea. I spent long hours investigating recipes that featured these super foods but would also prove easy on a chemo- and radiation-damaged constitution.

My goal was to fill my sister's freezer with a big variety of healthy, microwavable meals and treats to tempt her during the coming ordeal of chemotherapy and radiation treatments. The recipes I'd chosen included butternut squash and apple soup, roasted carrot and onion soup, and an African chicken with peanut butter and sweet potatoes. Meemee happily perched on the kitchen bar stool, reminded me of a baby bird as she willingly opened her mouth to be fed tastes of the various dishes I made for her approval.

Soon, all the ingredients had merged and disappeared into the many dishes I'd prepared. The freezer was neatly stacked with identical little microwave containers. I'd even made special Popsicles for the really bad days, having read they help the nausea and mouth problems. I flew home across the Pacific, feeling strong and capable, like I'd made a difference, hoping that the next months would be easy for my sister.

Halfway through the chemo treatments, The months I've been gone have not been easy. My sister's hair was gone, and she was battling some really horrible skin and body reactions to the chemo. I cooked some more—it was still the only thing I knew to do. My sister was so brave; she didn't complain even when we knew she was fighting the dizziness and scary pain. The side-effects of chemo are random and insidious and I hated what they were doing to her. I hated that I couldn't make the pain and weirdness go away. I cooked some more.

Finally, the ordeal was over. Nearly all the bad side effects we were warned of had occurred, but the cancer was gone, completely gone! All the food I made for my sister was gone now, too. Cooked with love, eaten with love, I can't believe it made a difference, and I'm just so happy she's all right. Now, I understand that the cancer may come back, but I'm sure in my heart that it won't. Every day Meemee is looking more like herself. Her hair has grown back; her body is recovering its shape; she's never looked more beautiful. She's also never been happier. There's nothing like almost losing your life to learn to appreciate each day.

Through her experience, I, too, am living every day with

more joy and meaning. Our whole family has finally let loose the collective breaths we've held for the past year. Every shared event is more appreciated now, as we realize how lucky we are to be together and relatively well. And I'm cooking with even more passion and commitment nowadays, convinced that healthy food will help keep my family cancer-free. There is one ingredient that can't be measured: *love*.

Below is a recipe that really made a difference for Meemee during the worst days after chemotherapy. The fruit and tofu provide both phytochemicals and much-needed protein and liquids, while the cool Popsicle soothed her sore mouth and settled her stomach.

Chemo Popsicles

Fresh-squeezed orange juice, one 8-ounce glass
Frozen mangoes, ¼ package, or 1 cup frozen berries
¼ square tofu, medium firmness
One banana
You can add passionfruit juice or other fruit juices to taste.

Put all ingredients into a blender. Blend to liquefy. Add more juice if it's too thick—it should be the thickness of a juice smoothie. Pour blended mixture into Tupperware or plastic Popsicle molds and freeze.

Barbara Curtis

All You Need Is Love

Love is a fruit in season at all times.

Mother Teresa

When people ask me, "How did you survive cancer?" I don't have to think twice. Bottom line? It was love—the love of God, as well as my patient, funny, rock-solid husband, Fred.

Poor Freddie never knew from one day to the next what kind of weird things stress was going to bring out in me, especially during those early weeks. But he hung in there because he loves me. I'll give you a "for instance."

One morning, I announced to my husband, "Hey, Freddie, I'm pretty sure I've figured out why I got breast cancer!"

He has learned by now to just say, "Okay," when I make an announcement like this. This time, he looked a little worried, but said, "Okay. . . ."

This is one of the reasons I love the guy so much. As far as I'm concerned, after twenty years with me, he's eligible for sainthood. I can't for the life of me figure out what I ever did to deserve him. Or, for that matter, what the poor guy ever did to deserve me! See, before I met Fred, I hadn't so much fallen in love as I'd stepped in it.

With the exception of my first love, Billy, in the sixth grade, and a few sweet but doomed relationships over the next thirteen years, my track record consisted mostly of men who thought I'd placed this ad in the personals: "Doormat seeking man to support. Only abusive, married, alcoholic, drug-addicted parolees need apply."

By the time Fred came along, I was a bitter twenty-six-year-old woman who believed there was nothing a man could do for me that a bottle of wine, a box of chocolates and an electric blanket couldn't do as well.

We met in Hawaii. I was vacationing; he was born and raised there.

Somewhere in my girlhood daydreams, I'd always pictured the man I'd end up happily married to some day. He'd be five to ten years older than me, six foot tall or better, have dark hair, and probably be a lawyer or doctor.

This just proves what I've always believed: God has a sense of humor. Freddie is six years younger than me, five foot six (to my five foot eight), has blond hair and was a struggling student (in engineering, not medical or law school) when I met him. In addition to all that, we were as different as oil and vinegar.

I knew it would never work. He was cuter than that proverbial bug's ear, smart, funny and willing to love me in spite of my rotten attitude, but it just wouldn't work. I kept telling him that, but he insisted it would and followed me home to Oregon. It took two years for me to figure out that oil and vinegar, while totally different, make a great salad dressing—something that clever Freddie had been trying to tell me all along. Finally realizing that I was in love with him was like seeing him through a clean pair of glasses.

You see, Freddie is a deep-rooted tree . . . and I'm a hummingbird flitting high overhead. He needs my bright colors and my outlook of the world . . . and I need the safety of his branches, the nurturing warmth of his leaves.

We got married and lived hopefully ever after.

So, as I was saying, my announcement of, "I think I've figured out why I got cancer!" was met with a wary, "Okay."

"It's my own fault, most likely."

He nodded, looking trapped.

"See, it all happened when I started to develop back in the sixth grade," I said. "Actually, it may even be my mother's fault."

"Your mother's fault?"

"She never told me about the development business, you know. I mean . . . how exactly the whole boob thing was going to come about," I said, frowning. "One day I woke up and there it was."

"There what was?"

"A lump!"

Fred looked confused, but waited to see where this was going.

"Yeah. One side had a lump. So my first thought was, *Oh, terrific, I have cancer!* But after the initial panic, I figured that maybe if I could flatten it back out, I'd be okay."

"Flatten it out?" My husband's mouth dropped open far enough to catch flies.

"Well, yeah! So I spent the next month or so pounding on it, mashing it against my desk at school—which, I wanna tell ya, got to be pretty darned painful after awhile—in the hopes that it would just give up and go away."

"You didn't!" Fred groaned, grimacing at the mental picture.

"Yup, I did. But not only didn't it go away, about the time when I'd convinced myself that it was a slow-growing kind of cancer and that maybe I could even live into my teens . . . it happened."

"What happened?"

"I woke up one morning and the OTHER side had a lump!"

My husband's eyebrows went up two-and-a-half inches. "The other side had a lump?"

I nodded seriously. "So I knew there was no way around it. I had to go tell my mom that I was dying. Of course, she handled it with all the sensitivity one would expect from their mother during a crisis like that: She laughed, and then explained about what was going on and how it wasn't unusual for girls' breast development to start on one side first."

Fred rolled his eyes and began massaging his temples.

"So I figure I probably discombobulated my DNA or something, pounding on myself like that! It's probably my own fault they're defective now." I sighed. "Guess I'll never know, huh?"

Fred just shook his head and stared at me for a long minute. Finally, he grinned and said, "I love you. You're about one raisin short of a fruitcake, but I love you."

See what I mean about him?

So like I said, when people ask, "How did you survive cancer? What's the one main thing that got you through?" this is what I tell them: "The Beatles definitely knew what they were talking about: 'All You Need Is Love.'"

Tina Wagner Mattern

"It may be the *closest* in proximity,
but it's not the *dearest* thing to my heart."

Reading *Charlotte's Web*

Each friend represents a world in us, a world possibly not born until they arrive, and it is only by this meeting that a new world is born.

Anaïs Nin

I spent the critical five years following my breast-cancer odyssey inspiring other women. I'd written a book that seemed to move people, and I was invited to speak at luncheons, fundraisers and celebrations all over the country. I'd dress up in my high heels and stockings, my skirts and jackets, wearing the fancy clothes like a shield against the thousands of stories that looked up at me from the audience. *You can have my story,* I was saying from the stage, *but I don't really want yours in return.*

People would rush up to me after my presentations wanting to tell tales of gloriously long survival or gut-wrenching death. I became expert at tuning them out. *Your sister died? I'm so sorry. Your mother survived? I'm so glad. You've just been diagnosed? Hang in there.* I'd say the same platitudes over and over again, not connecting, not engaging, not wanting to be part of the masses of women fighting this disease.

There was only one kind of story that pierced my armor like an arrow. I had been diagnosed when my children were three and six, and the only stories that I really heard during that entire period of time, the only ones that had any true resonance with me, were stories about young mothers who had died. The whole idea of it—how unfair, how terrifying, how harrowing, how awful—made me, the speech-giver, speechless.

How could anyone bear to die when their children were so young? What, exactly, would you do? How, exactly, would you proceed? My ears became greedy for these details, even though the immediate danger of death was passed for me. I wanted to know, and if anyone was willing to speak, I was ready to hear. I heard stories of young mothers who had written letters to their children before they died, made videos to record their life stories, even secured wives for their husbands. But I never heard exactly what I needed. I never heard exactly what I might do.

Then one day, I had just finished a speech in front of an audience of nearly one thousand people in Anchorage, Alaska. I made my way through the sea of survivors and was sitting at a table signing books and repeating my mantras . . . *I'm so sorry, I'm so glad, hang in there* . . . when a woman approached the table and told me her sister had recently died, leaving her to raise two little girls.

I froze. I had two little girls.

"What," I asked, as if it were the most natural thing to say to a stranger, "did your sister do in the end?"

The woman in front of me smiled. "She read her children *Charlotte's Web*."

Tears sprang to my eyes and to this woman's, too. I pictured her sister propped up in bed, her little girls snuggled next to her, the room darkened against the day and the night. I heard her voice— raspy, exhausted, desperate and strong—spinning the tale of love, loyalty and loss, and of the imperative for children to go out into the world and make their way. She sounded wise to me, this ghostly stranger.

"That," I said to the sister before me, "is exactly what I would do, too."

Jennie Nash

Locks of Love

What's important is finding out what works for you.

Henry Moore

The door flung open on the last day of school, and the children spilled out. I turned to begin organizing the books and sorting through papers when I noticed him just outside the door.

"Mrs. Cano, Mrs. Cano . . . don't you know me?" For a minute, I panicked. It's sometimes hard to recognize my former students as adolescents when the last time I'd seen them they were second-graders. How could I not know him?

"Daniel?" He was taller than I am now. He still wore glasses—and those incredible blue eyes!

Even as a first-year teacher, I could see he was a unique child. He had thick, long hair, golden and glistening, and his whole world was music. When I made him put away his music composition book during a lesson, Daniel never objected but would merely sigh with the resigned, all-knowing expression of an old man. This child was a genius, but he also had a unique sense of self, which was something I had been struggling with for years. How could I be "teaching" a child like this?

Daniel's hair was the ultimate symbol of his individuality. His mother came one day after school to explain that she was trying to get Daniel to agree to a haircut, but he had refused. It wasn't a defiant, tantrum-like refusal, his mother explained, but one that was grounded in his awareness of who he was. "He said he wouldn't be Daniel without it," she continued, and she confessed she just didn't have the heart to force him.

That was a year before I discovered the lump in my breast, a lump that progressed into my worst nightmare. I lost a year with the children, missed witnessing their growth and escapades. When I contemplate that year, I think of the endless succession of needles that delivered the poison that prolonged my life and brought me back to the classroom, to the children.

I lost my hair—all of it. It was humbling to see that alien looking back at me—no eyebrows, no eyelashes, no hair on her head. I felt invisible.

A few years later, a classmate of Daniel's ran up to me on the first day of school. "Mrs. Cano, did you see? Daniel cut his hair!"

What could have prompted him to relinquish the cherished trademark? I wondered. But he never told anyone why. No one insisted. They only wondered, and after a time, they never mentioned it because he didn't. He'd let that part of his identity go, but clearly, he was still Daniel.

Now, here he was, astonishingly grown up. "Just thought I'd come by and say hi," he said as he surveyed the room. "I remember I used to sit right over there," he gestured.

"Well, Daniel," I began, "now that you've graduated from eighth grade, do you have any idea what you want to be?"

I was startled to hear him say, "I want to be a professional skateboarder." He hesitated, "Or else study
accounting."

"But what happened to your music?" I asked.

He gave the familiar heavy sigh. "I don't know—maybe
I could do something with that, too."

It was a short conversation, and too soon, he was gone.
Just that morning, I was wondering if the children were
retaining anything I taught—not just academics, but other
things, such as how to make difficult decisions, understand different perspectives, distinguish between something significant and something that wasn't. Maybe
Daniel's visit was an answer to these questions.

Weeks later, I ran into Daniel's mother at the supermarket. We exchanged niceties, and I told her how thrilled I
felt to see Daniel again. Then I said, "I didn't think he
would EVER cut his hair. I guess he just outgrew the need
for it."

"Oh," his mother responded, "didn't he tell you? It was
because of you—he did it because of you. The hair went to
the Children's Cancer Foundation for wigs."

Leah Cano
As previously appeared in
Mamm Magazine

2

SUPPORT

*There is no support so strong as the strength
that enables one to stand alone.*

Ellen Glasgow

He Doesn't Take "No" for an Answer

Live life more fully, love more unconditionally and trust in the goodness of life.

Susan B. Komen Newsletter, Houston, Texas

A child's optimism should send a message to us all. My eleven-year-old's response to my breast-cancer recurrence was more than I could ever have anticipated.

My children had only known me as a survivor because I had spent six and a half years in remission. I had always feared a relapse, and one of my great concerns was how my children would react and cope if the cancer returned, because now they were old enough to understand so much more.

In February 2001, I was diagnosed with metastatic breast cancer, with additional disease in my liver and bones. I began extensive chemotherapy treatments, and my physical condition worsened before it stabilized. Living with these changes were my husband and two sons.

A friend was walking in the Avon three-Day, sixty-Mile Breast Cancer Walk, and Andrew, my eleven-year-old, decided he would hold a fund-raising dance at the local recreation center for sixth-grade students and donate all the proceeds to the walk. He took command of the task and pulled all the details together after he asked my husband to take care of renting the room at the recreation center for the night. Andrew set out to solicit donations, and enlisted the services of a disc jockey and his brother's band as entertainment. A friend's mom donated the soda, candies and goodies, and he asked adults to chaperone the party.

The dance was a great success, and $2,000 was raised. A *Boston Globe* reporter interviewed him, and an article followed. Soon, donations flowed in from the greater Boston community. One person sent tickets to an NSYNC concert, which were sold to the highest bidder. All this raised another $2,000, also donated to the Avon Fund.

To date, Andrew has held two more annual dances that raised thousands of dollars for the Memorial Sloane-Kettering and Massachusetts General Hospital's Breast Cancer Research Centers. He now is the disc jockey for the dances, advertises for the events, places donation boxes at local businesses and has become quite the entrepreneur for charity events.

Living with cancer has become part of our everyday lives, and as my survival continues, the boys have grown accustomed to my life and live like normal kids. We all understand it is important to live each day—with the emphasis on *living*, not just surviving. The lessons learned are real, not from video games.

We all know that life isn't fair. Some face war and famine; some deal with poverty and crime; others face illness . . . and all of us have to accept our current conditions, fight our battles and look forward with hope for the future.

Recently, the cancer has progressed to my brain. After a number of stereostatic surgeries, whole and partial brain radiation treatments and continuing chemotherapy, our family continues to fight the battle.

This spring, Andrew was given the Principal's Award at the eighth-grade commencement, honored in part for his continuing community service and breast cancer fund-raising activities. Of course, we were very proud when the principal said, "He is a leader among his classmates, particularly in service-oriented projects. When he feels passionate about something, Andrew doesn't take no for an answer." It was also noted that "he is guided to make the world a better place."

He has certainly made my world a better one!

Ellen B. Leavitt

Giving and Receiving

People believe that food cures. Couscous, asparagus, baked chicken, turkey soup, macaroni and cheese, chocolate pudding, cornbread, broiled salmon, lasagna, tacos, strawberry smoothies—all arrived on my doorstep, unbidden, like manna from heaven, during the time I needed wound care.

They came from women in the neighborhood and women at church, from mothers of Carlyn's classmates and the director of Emily's preschool. Sometimes they came four at a time, food piling up as though we were getting ready for a party or an earthquake. Each night, Rob and the girls and I would sit down to complete, hot, precooked meals, and for a few moments, pretend as though life was normal.

Taking a meal to someone is such a primal act. Even in our microwavable, take-out, drive-through world, it survives, like a flower pushing through the cracks in the cement. People can't do anything to help the fact that you have cancer in your breast or a wound across your abdomen, but they can drive you to the hospital every morning if you can't drive yourself, and they can do something about the fact that you will be hungry at the end of the day—and they do.

At first, I cringed at so much goodwill. I knew some of the mothers had problems of their own, yet they brought me gifts to make my life easier. I felt as if goodwill were a bank account I was depleting, casserole by casserole. How would I ever pay them all back?

It was Cassi, a twelve-year-old girl, the eldest child in a family with five children, who showed me that payment wasn't the point.

Cassi didn't believe much in the curative power of food. She put her faith in babysitting and volunteered to stay with our children, Carlyn and Emily, while my husband, Rob, and I went to our cancer support groups every Tuesday night for twelve weeks. She folded our girls' doll clothes, put the picture books back on the bookshelf and helped Carlyn study for her spelling tests—and wouldn't let us pay her a dime. I tried to be coy and slide the money into her back pocket, but she shook her head and said, "No, thank you. I don't want to be paid."

I took my case to her mother, thinking I was doing a good deed for a kid who wouldn't stand up for herself. Her mother said, "That's what we've counseled her to say," and I rearranged my thoughts to see that Cassi was only doing what her parents thought was proper.

"But that's not fair to Cassi," I argued. "She's giving us a ton of time."

"It was her idea," her father explained, changing the picture in my mind yet again. "She's been looking for a service project she could really do herself, with her own talents, and you're it. We're going to continue to instruct her to refuse your money because we want to support her effort."

I glanced at Cassi, who was twisting her hair in the doorway. I thought, *I'm a service project? I'm in bad enough shape to be a service project?*

"Think how few chances a twelve-year-old has to

serve," Cassi's mom explained. But instead of thinking of a twelve-year-old's reality, I thought of my friend, Lisa, who had recently died, and how much I'd wanted to take enchiladas to her home for her family, and how much I wanted to take her boys to the park, and how I hadn't been able to do those things for her.

I promised Cassi I wouldn't pay her until I felt well again. I didn't pay her until late February when, instead of a doctor's appointment or a cancer support group, Rob and I went out for dinner. Only then would she accept money and a card from us, telling her how much she had supported and given to our family.

Jennie Nash

Reprinted with permission of Allan Hirsh ©1990.

Little Man Christopher

The Child is father to the Man.

William Wordsworth

Upon receiving my diagnosis of aggressive breast cancer, my husband, Tony, and I were faced with the challenge
of how to deal with the situation without frightening our
son, Christopher, who had just turned three. He was
already trying to adjust to having a new baby in the house
and being a big brother to six-month-old Emily, and he
didn't need any more burdens on his little shoulders.

We decided not to try and explain the frightening ordeal
we were embarking on, but to go about our business, trying to keep daily life as routine as possible for the sake of
the children. This worked to a point, but eventually things
like prolonged illness, fatigue and loss of hair gave
Christopher the impression that all wasn't well at our
house.

"Mommy's very sick," I finally said to him, after he had
noticed I was different. "My body is trying to fight the
sickness, and that's why all my hair fell out. Don't worry,

though . . . when I feel better, it will all grow back."

After having said that, I wondered if I had done the right thing. One day, when Christopher had a tummy ache, he asked, "Will my hair come out, too?" And when little Emily had a fever, he expected her hair to come out as well.

So on we went, through months of chemotherapy. The schedule was the same each time: take the children to school, have a treatment, sleep until they come home, and back to work by Monday. Between treatments, Tony gave me Neupogen injections to keep my white cell count up. This ensured I could have my next treatment without a slip in the schedule.

I'll never forget the first time Christopher heard me get sick after a treatment. I thought I was being so discreet, first opening the bedroom door and slipping quietly into the master bathroom, then closing the door behind me and letting loose. All of a sudden, out of nowhere, there was his little hand rubbing my back oh-so-gently. "It's okay, Mommy," he'd say to me.

After seeing me in such a vulnerable position, he found it difficult to leave my side. Many a night, his daddy carried him to bed after he fell asleep while comforting me. Many a day, we struggled to separate from each other when dropping him off at preschool.

I'll always remember and cherish the moment he first discovered my hair was growing back. He came to my room, and a look of wonder came over his face as he caught sight of me. "Are you feeling better today, Mommy?"

Without thinking much about it, I replied that I was doing all right. "I knew it!" he said with a big grin. "It's coming back!" With that, my little man gently rubbed my head for the first of many times throughout my recovery.

Since then, we've finished chemotherapy, radiation,

numerous surgeries, and endured several years of hormone therapy. It's hard to say whether Christopher, now eleven years old, has any recollection of that period or not. I'm sure he isn't aware of how serious things really were, as we were very careful not to use the "c" word in our house back then.

It's funny how, as parents, we go through every day, constantly faced with challenges we didn't expect, without a handbook, and often making important decisions on the spur of the moment. Our choice to provide our son with something tangible to help him understand our crisis was, I believe, the right one. To this day, he always tells me that I have pretty hair, and I wonder if somewhere in the back of his mind, he's subconsciously harboring the memory of that difficult period of time.

We've always expected to be there for our children, to provide support and help them through life's challenges. What we never counted on was the amount of strength we would draw from them, and just how big a role this little man would play in bringing our family through the most difficult of times. Thank you, Christopher.

Kathy Vancura

Debbie's Story

What comes from the heart, goes to the heart.

Samuel Taylor Coleridge

I had belonged to the cancer support group for three years, and Debbie had never been a regular attendee. In the advanced stages of ovarian cancer, she had too many places to go, people to meet and experiences to undergo.

But we always looked forward to her return, and after each adventure, Debbie would report back to the group.

"Ayers Rock is as amazing as I had hoped it would be," she effused after her trip to Australia. "It was my dream to see it before I died." And she brought out her photos and her stories and her smile. Debbie had a smile as wide as any room she entered. It is still my strongest memory of her.

I don't think I ever knew what Debbie really did for a living, but someone once suggested she might have been a model. Even in her illness, she was beautiful. Or maybe that was her smile. Anyway, it didn't really matter.

We never spent a lot of time at our meetings talking about the past. The present was too all-consuming for each of us.

Debbie was by no means the only member of our group who was facing her own death. Some traveled, like Debbie, braving exotic locations in spite of physical weaknesses or colostomy bags or post-treatment fatigue. Some stayed at home and made the most of remaining time with family and friends. Some were resigned, some philosophical, some fearful as they came to terms with their mortality. Death is a personal thing. But Debbie's way was my favorite: facing it full-on, with verve and spunk and gusto and joy. On the night she announced she was leaving the city and moving to a hospice that would let her be nearer her family, I knew we would never see her again, and it left an empty place in my heart.

On a cold and dreary winter evening, one of our members reported her phone call to Debbie's hospice. Surrounded by her family, Debbie was close to death. Her kidneys had failed, but in the final hours of her life, she still managed to take a brief phone call. She wished us all well. That had been several days before, so we knew she was gone. During the meeting, we lit a candle and had a moment's silence in memory of our friend.

Two weeks later, Debbie appeared in the doorway of our meeting room. Thinner, weaker, walking with a crutch, she was assisted to a chair by her sister. "Hi," she beamed. "Bet you didn't expect me tonight!" We stared at her, stunned.

Debbie laughed. "Who (besides doctors) says doctors know it all, anyway?" she gushed. "There I was, at death's door and beyond, and suddenly, for some reason, my kidneys kicked into gear. Go figure." And she laughed again.

Her laughter waned. "I can't stay long. I have to get back. It's just, I know some of you are facing what I face, and I had to come tell you, it's all right. I was there, you see. In fact, I feel cheated I had to come back. And it's beautiful there, wherever it is. Then, all of a sudden, here I am again." She shrugged. "I had to come and tell you all: Don't be afraid. You're going to be okay."

I don't remember what happened after that. We all said good-bye, like we would see her next week. We knew we wouldn't.

At our next meeting, we lit a candle for Debbie once again. During our moment of silence, I thought of her smile, and her warmth and joy. Debbie had given us her last report on her biggest journey.

Lolly Susi

Science Mom

Your first emotion isn't, "Am I going to lose my breast?" It's, "Am I going to lose my life?"

Linda Ellerbee

Telling people I had breast cancer was something I dreaded. Why? Because I was afraid of their reaction—that it would weaken me, that we would both cry, that we would fall apart. Most of all, I was worried to tell my parents.

Luckily, I was guided by Ted, a wise friend who had been through the journey before. He had lost his first wife to cancer, and he was well-versed in the strange and separate world that one enters after hearing the words, "You have cancer."

"Keep it simple," he said. "Stick to the facts."

He urged me to find out the exact medical terminology for my type of cancer and use those terms when describing it to people for the first time. "If it's a small ductal carcinoma, the easiest type to treat,' then that's what you should say."

I practiced saying it a few times until it rolled off my

tongue easily. I called my mother even though I was very
worried about what her reaction might be. I didn't want to
scare her, or have her fall apart.

"Hi, Mother, I have some news about my recent mammogram I need to tell you. They found a small ductal carcinoma, the easiest type to treat, with the best success
rates."

I waited for her terrified response. To my utter shock,
her reaction was quite the opposite—she was wonderful.
She just listened, then asked intelligent questions, and
then asked more questions about the scientific aspects.
She became "science mom." It was great.

Gradually, I became aware that I come from a family of
strength. I got this image of my family of strong but feminine women, of which I'm a part. I don't know what I
thought my mother would say—she had always been
strong in crises, and I felt really confident after talking to
her. I told her it would be okay to tell everyone—in fact, I
would welcome it. My fear of telling others turned out to
be nonsense because everybody has been fantastic—very
strong and calm.

And I know that Ted's advice made it possible for all of
us to pass through this frightening phase of the emotional
and medical journey of breast cancer. Knowledge is
power, and the ability to simplify and understand the
enemy made it easier for me, my family and friends to deal
with it. He gave the fear a name, and when something has
a name it is robbed of its power.

Mary Olsen Kelly

Enjoy Life!

Time: consoler of affliction and softener of anger.

Charles Dickens

Ann kept saying, "Look two years down the road." But what was I supposed to be looking at? I was sick, tired and scared. The future was uncertain, and the road ahead looked endless and filled with so many obstacles. *Can my body hold up? Do I have enough inner strength and faith in God to meet this challenge? Will I find sunshine and happiness at the end?* I didn't know the answers, but when I felt my eight-year-old's hand in mine, I knew I had to "look two years down the road."

Ann was a friend of my husband's family, and when she heard I had cancer, she suggested we get a second opinion. The answer was the same: chances were fifty/fifty that my cancer would come back. But she didn't give up and got me an appointment with a private doctor who was one of the best in the country. He suggested I go through some stronger chemotherapy in five months and predicted I'd do well. He gave me a better chance of surviving and believed I'd live to a ripe, old age. Hope came like a sunrise.

And I had Ann: "Don't believe statistics, because no two cancer patients are alike." I thought, *If four out of ten people survive longer than five years, then I'm going to be one of those four people.* I visualized that I was healthy, and the cancer cells were disappearing. I did this every day.

My will to survive strengthened every time I looked at my sons. My older son was fifteen, and I knew he still needed me to help him over some of the bumps in life. My younger son was eight, and he needed me more than anyone else. I remember praying that God would give me just ten more years to live so I could see my younger son graduate from high school.

Finally, one day I got tired of living in fear. I got angry! I remember thinking: *If I am going to die and no one knows when that's going to be, then I'm going to enjoy the time I have left!* I realized that if I did live a long time, I'd end up being mad at myself for wasting so much of my life when I could have been enjoying it. A nurse told me when I first started chemo, "I believe that when your job on Earth is done, only then will you die." I thought this was a wonderful outlook on life, and I began to feel the same way.

I honestly believe these thoughts were the real turning points in my fight against cancer. I started on the long journey to continue conditioning my mind to stop worrying about when I was going to die and started to live one day at a time. It took a lot of mental training to overcome my fears, but soon days turned into weeks, and weeks turned into months, and I was still here. I knew there would still be bad days ahead, but I now had the inner strength to deal with them.

Ann was right—it took two years for me to complete my treatments and feel better. There were still occasional days when I was afraid, especially when I had to have a bone scan or blood work done to see if the cancer was still in remission.

Underneath it all, I was amazed and awed by the way my life had turned out. I saw my younger son graduate from high school—an emotional day for me. I felt remarkably well and was doing things I had never dreamed I'd be able to do: laughing again, working a full-time job and watching my family grow up.

What would I tell someone fighting cancer? Look two years down the road—when your treatments are done, your hair has grown back, and your body has recovered. Believe that you are going to beat the odds even when it doesn't seem possible. I did. Persevere. There were times I was utterly exhausted and wanted to give up, but I knew my family needed me.

Find the reason you need to survive and hold onto it. Don't worry about dying. That is in God's hands. Just live and be grateful for each joy, each day.

Regina Dodson

Filler

The happiest moments of my life have been the few which I have passed at home in the bosom of my family.

Thomas Jefferson

My husband and I went to Paducah, Kentucky, one Thanksgiving to meet with our son and his family, who had come from Florida. They stayed in a motel with an indoor swimming pool.

After spending Thanksgiving Day with the family, the grandkids wanted to go swimming. My oldest grandson Harrison, age six, asked, "Granny, can you come swim with me?"

"Yes," I said, and I got my swimsuit, prosthesis and a towel. Off we went.

Now, this swimsuit was not made for breast-cancer women, so I got on my bathing suit and put the prosthesis in the cup of the suit. We walked down to the pool, jumped in and swam to the steps. Harrison got out first and turned around to help me.

His eyes got as big as saucers as his jaw dropped. He

pointed at me and said, "Grandma, did you come from another planet?"

I looked down to where he was pointing and saw that my prosthesis had come out of the cup and had slid down to my belly button.

"I've come a long way," I answered.

Bonnie Seibert

Heart Massage

The first time I met Jeanie, she was walking down the path in front of my apartment, and I was walking toward her. I noticed that she was wearing a pink ribbon, and I was wearing mine, too. I stopped in front of her and said, "Wow, looks like we have something in common."

She was taken aback and replied, "What do you mean?"

"Well, you're wearing your pink ribbon and so am I. Do you know someone who was diagnosed with breast cancer?"

"Yes," she whispered. "Me." She walked away quickly.

I'm a licensed massage therapist, and in my work over the years I have seen many people in pain. Recently, I have been seeing a lot of women with breast cancer.

A few days later I received a phone call from Jeanie's husband. I had given him a massage the year before, when they visited my island home.

"I'd like to give my wife a massage as a gift and surprise her. She said she met you yesterday and had a good feeling about you."

When Jeanie walked into my massage room a few days later, she seemed tense and angry. It was a warm, beautiful day, and her treatment had been a gift from her husband, so I was puzzled why she was upset.

A gift for you

As you may remember, these books changed my life and made me who I am today. I haven't happened to read this particular one, but I hope that these stories are meaningful to you. I LOVE YOU SO MUCH!!!!!!!!!!!!! - Marty

"Are you feeling well?" I asked.

"My back hurts, and I'm a little nauseous."

And yet she was here and wanted to have her body massaged. I left the room, as I always do, to give her privacy for changing clothes and positioning herself on the massage table.

After I got her situated, the bed adjusted and my hands washed, I began by resting one hand at the base of her neck and the other on her lower back, allowing us both to become quiet.

In a calm voice, I suggested, "Let your eyes close and bring your attention to your breath." After several minutes, I applied warmed lotion and gave light, delicate stroking motions to her back and neck. I used long, slow movements to soothe her and encourage rest.

As I give a massage, I remind myself that there is nothing to "fix." I need only to "be present" with the person who is going through discomfort.

As soon as I turned her over onto her back, her breathing became ragged, and she began to cry. I let her cry quietly for a while, and then asked, "Would you like me to incorporate mental imagery into the session?" She nodded.

"You can soften the discomfort you're feeling and be open to it rather than push it away." That was all. No other words. Just "open" and "soften."

At the end of the treatment, as I was holding and stretching her neck, she began sobbing. I continued holding her without comment, allowing her a safe place to cry, to release, to heal.

While Jeanie was getting dressed, she quietly but firmly said, "I would like to reschedule at least one more treatment with you while I'm here in Maui. I recently had a double mastectomy. As part of my healing process, I tried massage, but the therapist was clinical and cold, and the massage was painful and traumatic. I was terrified to get

another treatment—and that's why I was so upset when I
came here.

"I can't begin to tell you how much lighter in body and
spirit I feel right now. And so connected! At the risk of crying all over again, I want to let you know how much you
have helped me today to take that first huge step back
toward allowing another human being to touch me . . .
without fear or shame or remorse! Thank you!"

It is an honor to be able to perform this type of healing
work, and I was filled with a profound sense of grace and
warmth. Light filled me. A completely transformed woman
emerged from the massage session, and another transformed woman prepared her massage studio for the next
client.

Pandora Kurth

My Heroes

*Believe that life is worth living, and your belief
will help create that fact.*

William James

"Hero"—a word that is misused and often overused in
today's society. We make instant media heroes of people
for acts that should be expected from one person to
another. Young boys believe you're a hero if you make
millions and can play a sport better than someone else.
Young girls feel the same way about celebrities and measure their worth by this invalid yardstick.

Some special people are heroes to me: I met them at the
local cancer center while going through treatments for
breast cancer. I entered with an open mind and didn't
know what to expect. What I discovered were people who
constantly amazed me. I met them at different stages in
their cancers. Some were at the end of treatment, knowing
that cancer would win the battle. Others, more fortunate,
whose disease was caught in time and treated, had hope
of a long or permanent remission. I met women and men

who, while suffering through chemotherapy and radiation, never lost their sense of humor. Some had young families, and some were grandparents.

In a room filled with all these troubles, I met my heroes. Each day I found new friends who loved life and loved to laugh . . . people whose diseases took much, but never broke their spirit or took the laughter from their lives. In the waiting room, we joked about our lives beyond our illness, and our laughter often echoed all the way down the hall. We celebrated when each of us had our last radiation treatment, and we hugged each other good-bye when it was time "to graduate." We also supported each other when problems occurred. At one point, I was burned by the radiation, and my fellow patients brought me through. I have been incredibly blessed by family, friends and fellow patients.

These are my heroes—ordinary, extraordinary beings who live life and are grateful for every new day, who have the compassion to care for their families and each other while battling cancer. My prayer is that their remissions are permanent and their lives are long and joyous.

Maria McNaught

"Tweety Conquers That Mean Old Bweast Cancer"

I attribute my success to this—I never gave or took any excuse.

Florence Nightingale

We all have some type of "guardian angel" that watches over us. Mine happens to be Tweety Bird. Many years ago, I was told I looked like Tweety because of my spiky, blonde haircut and big blue eyes. Over the years, Tweety became a "mascot" of sorts, but when I was diagnosed with breast cancer in October 1996, Tweety quickly assumed a more important role in my life.

Because there was a history of breast cancer on my mom's side, I can't say I was totally surprised to get my news. I was three months shy of my "BIG 50."

There is no "right" way to receive this news, but my OB/GYN for thirty-plus years should probably be the poster boy for how NOT to tell a woman she has breast cancer. He called me at my office (after trying me at home, and scaring my husband and mother half to death). A man of few words, he said, "I have the results of your biopsy, and it's malignant, so you need to do something quickly."

Well, what I quickly did was hang up the phone, walk into a staff member's office, state "I have breast cancer" (which really made it REAL), and burst into tears. I added, "I can't do this!"

She immediately replied, "Yes, you can, and you will." Two of my staff members drove me home, where my husband and mom were anxiously waiting.

Those weren't the last tears I shed, but it was the last time I said "I can't" through the entire ordeal.

Once I got over the initial shock of actually having breast cancer, I went into immediate action by creating a notebook entitled "Tweety's Battle with (and VICTORY OVER) Bweast Cancer." I divided it into four sections: (1) Lumpectomy or Mastectomy? (2) Reconstruction Options; (3) Treatment Options; and (4) General Information. Using information that I obtained from the Internet, various books and the Y-ME Breast Cancer Support Group, I created a list of "interview questions" for each specialist I was going to be seeing. This research helped educate me, and there is no doubt in my mind that knowledge truly is power! As the vice president of human resources for my company, I've had extensive experience in developing training manuals and conducting managerial training on how to conduct interviews. Little did I know I would be applying this knowledge personally. My doctors were impressed—and often amused—during my "interviews." By injecting humor at every possible opportunity, I approached breast cancer head-on with a strength and determination that even amazed me!

As a result of my Q&A sessions, I came away from each appointment with more knowledge, which allowed me to make the decisions that were right for me. I opted for a mastectomy, with five years on tamoxifen and tissue-expansion reconstruction—a lengthy process that resulted in a new nickname at my office: "Dolly Darke" (after the large-busted celebrity Dolly Parton). My doctors still laugh when they remember how I was trying to talk them into liposuction and a face lift as I was being wheeled into the operating room, wearing a Tweety pin on my surgical gown.

After my surgery, I became a certified volunteer with Y-ME, manning the twenty-four-hour Hopeline and serving as a "match" for newly diagnosed women. I also wrote a letter to the *Washington Post*, which was published, and to my Virginia congressmen, protesting "drive-through mastectomies."

I vividly remember one woman for whom I was a match. She was from another country and had no family and very few friends in the United States. She was scheduled for a double mastectomy, and her HMO was planning to send her home alone the day of her surgery. Appalled, I contacted the hospital and her insurance carrier and made arrangements for her to remain in the hospital for two nights. They even had a health-care representative go to her home and check on her after she was released.

We had talked by phone many times, but had never met. The day after her surgery, I burst into her hospital room to visit her and brought butterfly balloons—in Y-ME the butterfly signifies "new beginnings"—and a card. She was so tiny and looked so alone and forlorn in this huge bed. When I introduced myself, her eyes lit up, and she clapped her hands like an excited child!

As I mentioned earlier, I have a very short, spiky haircut, and her first comment to me was, "Is your hair just growing back?"

I responded with a laugh, "No, my hair always looks like this!"

She was very apprehensive about her scheduled reconstruction, not understanding the process, so I just opened my suit jacket and showed her my finished results. She was reassured and relieved. After my visit, I truly felt as though I had made a difference in her recovery process.

Today, more than seven cancer-free years later, I recently re-experienced the many emotions (shock, fear, anger, acceptance, determination) when my older sister was diagnosed with breast cancer at sixty-one. I dusted off my Tweety Bird notebook and headed to Richmond, Virginia, to ensure that my "guardian angel" was available if needed.

The amazing experiences that I've had and the incredible survivors who I have been so blessed to know since my initial diagnosis have had a tremendously positive impact on my life.

All serve to reinforce the motto of Y-ME: "No woman should ever have to go through breast cancer alone."

Susan Darke

"We're all in this together."

Blessed by Friends

Love cures people, both the ones who give it and the ones who receive it.

Dr. Karl Menninger

"Cancer"—it is such an ugly word that people tend to shy away from it. That was my belief until the past few months.

I am a single mother with breast cancer that has metastasized to my liver. For anyone who is not familiar with the disease, let me tell you that the co-pays, prescriptions and treatments are astronomically expensive. I have been going through treatments for some time now and found myself not knowing how I could continue to make ends meet. I am a very proud person and refused to let anyone know my situation or ask for help.

What I didn't know was that the whole time I was struggling over how, what and when to pay, everyone at work was aware of my situation. I've been employed at the same office for almost sixteen years. It turns out they were having bake sales, raffles, hot-dog sales, collections, you name it . . . and all the proceeds were given to me!

I was also given a large donation from someone who does not even work with me, who prefers to remain anonymous.

Now with the blessings of all my friends and those I don't even know, I no longer am struggling. I have been able to buy some Christmas presents for my children and grandchildren. I even have money set aside for my next rounds of chemo and prescriptions.

I truly believe that God is watching out for me. He is doing that through the blessings of friends.

Judy Hague

The Glow Girls

Where there is laughter, there is always more health than sickness.

Phyllis Bottome

The lives of four women were changed forever the fall of 1999. These women did not meet on the golf course, the country club or bowling league. They met at the Blood and Cancer Center in Canfield, Ohio, and the bond that brought them to that building on Tuesday mornings was cancer. These four women were young wives with children, going to work every day and enjoying life to the fullest.

Tuesday mornings brought them together because all were receiving chemotherapy. It had started with a friendly smile and a hello. Lynn and Karen were the first two to introduce themselves to each other. It just so happened they sat next to each other that first day as chemo was dripping through their veins. They knew they were going to be there for a while, so they befriended each other and started a conversation. Soon they became chemo friends, discovered they were on the same treatment schedule and knew they would be seeing much of each other. A month later, Sandy arrived in the chemo room and decided to take the chair next to Lynn and Karen. Soon after that, Cindy came into the picture, and now they are the Fearless Foursome.

The circle of four was there once a month on Tuesday, and the nurses reserved their four chairs for them. They would sit and compare their bald heads; someone from the group would bring snacks to be shared; someone was always telling a funny story. There was always laughter coming from the chemo room when these ladies were together. You never knew what the Fearless Four were going to do next; when these women were together, it was one crazy party! One time there was so much laughter, the doctor walked into the room to see what all the noise was about.

Having fun and laughing is contagious—often other chemo patients joined in the fun. The Fearless Foursome did very well throughout treatment, and it must have been the laughter. When one of them finished her cancer treatments, she would have a graduation party—the graduation party of life. There would be pizza, pop and cake for everyone. Gifts, balloons and flowers would adorn the chemo room. Party hats were worn on bald heads. Once someone brought in a bottle of wine, and the girls had a tiny sip out of a bathroom Dixie cup.

The funny four are no longer meeting at chemo; they have taken their laughter and now meet at a restaurant for lunch. They have decided it's important for them to stay in touch; after all, they've spent their last six months together, running the race of life.

Many months have passed, and the four decided it was time to do something more—to reach out to other women living with cancer. They realize how important it is to love and encourage others, and they formed a support group called The Glow Girls. They always said, "If we're in a room together with the lights out, we would surely glow!"

Actually, Glow Girls stands for Gracious, Loving, Optimistic Women living with cancer. They are not counselors; they are friends. Women need to know there is life after cancer. These ladies do not offer medical advice; what they do offer is love, encouragement and friendship. They'll tell you what it's like to lose your hair, and they'll also tell you about their beautiful new hair. They will answer questions a newly diagnosed patient might have. These women tell all cancer survivors to be strong, stay positive and make sure you laugh along the way.

Today there are more than thirty Glow Girls. Was it by chance that these four ladies met? No way! God had a plan. None of these women would wish cancer on anyone, but through their cancer experience they have become different people. If it hadn't been for cancer, this friendship would never have occurred.

The circle of four is now a large circle, still laughing and having great fun. Cancer has been part of their lives, but they took a negative event and turned it into a positive experience. You'll know when the Glow Girls are together—just follow their laughter.

Karen Theis

Bring on the Lasagna!

Strange to see how a good dinner and feasting reconciles everybody.

Samuel Pepys

There must be some healing properties in lasagna; ask anyone who has ever been sick or in need about all the lasagna that suddenly appears in their life.

After Ian brought me home from the hospital following my mastectomy, we found the principal and a fellow teacher sitting on our front lawn. After hugs and tears of joy, the principal said, "I've brought dinner for your family." We were very grateful for the homemade meat lasagna, especially since it lasted for two meals.

The next lasagna came from my classroom. I had been fortunate enough to be able to teach my third-grade class through almost six months of chemotherapy.

My room mother showed up after school with a large bag. Inside were meals for my family purchased from a popular Italian restaurant in our area: two lasagnas, one meat and one vegetarian.

I believe the third, fourth and fifth lasagnas came from

church. Before the start of chemotherapy, someone from the Women's Ministry called and told us that various church members would provide our family with meals. The food would be left inside the refrigerator in the church kitchen, and we could pick it up at our convenience. The meals could be kept in our freezer and reheated, which really helped out during those times when I was just too weak or sick to cook. We enjoyed homemade meatballs, chicken casserole . . . and lots of lasagna!

Maybe the ancient Italians put in some secret ingredient akin to whatever Grandma puts in the chicken soup. The "healing properties" of lasagna must have worked because I have been cancer free ever since.

Lorna Maxwell

"The road of life isn't ALL about shopping . . .
there are a few pit stops for love and
chocolate along the way!"

Reprinted with permission of Stephanie Piro ©2005.

Family Scenes

Let us, then, be up and doing, with a heart for any fate.

Henry Wadsworth Longfellow

From the day my first child was born, I did everything I could to protect and comfort him. It was like a crusade. I picked him up the second he cried; I watched him sleep. I baby-proofed my home, and there are still some cabinets I can't open. Protecting my child and keeping him safe was my mission in life.

As he got older, he would fall down and bump something or other, but I was always there with the necessary Band-aid and kiss. When we went to the doctor for a shot, I would let him squeeze my hand tight until it was over. Then he would get a sticker. That was the deal, and we never broke it.

When I was diagnosed with cancer, my first thoughts were, *Who will take care of my children? Who is going to protect them?* My husband and I sat them down and gave them as much information as we thought a three and five-year-old could handle. We talked about the surgery and the hospital and the medication that would make Mommy's hair fall out. We made sure they had "sleepovers" at Grandma's house when I had my treatments so they wouldn't see Mommy so sick.

What I hadn't expected and didn't explain to the kids were the Neupogen shots. I hadn't realized that my white blood count would be so low that I'd require it with every treatment. I would wake every morning before the kids and give myself the shot, or my husband would do it when they weren't around, but Nathan, our five-year-old, who doesn't miss a trick, caught on.

One morning when I went to give myself the shot, there he was. He took my hand in his and said, "You can squeeze it as tight as you like until it's over, and then you can have a sticker. That's the deal." So I held his hand, gave myself the shot, and he proudly put a sticker on my shirt. It was then I realized that, for as much as I wanted to protect and comfort my children, they wanted to do the same for me. I was so glad to have them take care of me!

Before I started chemotherapy, my husband and children shaved my head. We thought it would make it easier for them to deal with my hair loss. We went shopping and picked out hats and scarves for me to wear. Our son insisted that I wear my hat whenever we were out, and I always did. One day the doorbell rang, and without thinking, I opened the door without my hat on! Three of Nathan's friends were standing there and started laughing and calling me "baldy," but Nathan was devastated and embarrassed. I explained to him that it didn't bother me, and we should laugh it off like a joke. They were kids. They didn't understand, and besides, I was pretty bald.

A few weeks later, we were at the pool—my husband, myself and the two children. I, of course, had my hat on. Nathan wanted me to come into the water. I told him I'd have to take off my hat. He didn't seem to mind. While we

were playing in the water, a few of his friends came in.
One went up to him and said, "Hey, Nathan, is that your
mom?"

"Yeah," he replied.

"She's bald."

"Yeah, I know. The good news is, her hair will grow
back. The bad news is, my Dad's won't."

My slightly balding husband and I have never laughed
so hard. Nathan was able to see some humor in the situation, and so were we.

Ruth Kotler

Joining the Race

The longer we dwell on our misfortunes, the greater is their power to harm us.

Voltaire

As the sun hovered over Cocalico's football field, hundreds of people gathered around the campus. Some were finishing their meals under the bright yellow tent; many were on the track, while others were starting to make their way onto the bleachers. The first lap of the American Cancer Society's Relay for Life was about to begin—a race against cancer, full of people determined to make a difference, including my mom. There she stood on the track, ready to lead the survivor lap.

Since my aunt and uncle sponsored the survivor lap, my entire family participated in it. My mom was radiant that evening. Her energy was contagious, her smile uplifting, and her pride evident. It was obvious she was reflecting on the past year and what she had endured.

Although the past year was still on my mind, my thoughts were focused on the present. Behind me people continued to gather on the track. They were the survivors.

I chuckled as the event organizers scrambled to make sure every survivor was wearing a pin. There was no need for some emblem on this night. Their expressions clearly told everyone, *I am a survivor!* Mixed in with the smiles, laughter and hugs, there were tears. The tears simply added to the atmosphere.

The lap was about to begin when I looked over at my mom and smiled; she returned the favor. There was a time not too long ago when my mother wasn't thinking about some relay. Then again, there was a time not too long before that when my mother wasn't even thinking about cancer. But now it was all she could think about. We started the march to the ribbon signifying the start of the lap.

That lap was memorable, no doubt about it. Chills ran down my spine when we turned the last corner and saw the bleachers filled with spectators. The standing ovation they gave was genuine—there was nothing scripted about it. Again, I glanced over at my mom and smiled; there was nothing scripted about that either.

The impact cancer has had on our society is great; the impact it has had on my family is even greater. For over a year, my mother endured the physical and emotional effects of cancer. Her tribulations left her tired, yet determined.

As I walked off the track following the survivor lap, I felt my mother's determination. I realized we weren't gathered there to *start* some monumental race against cancer; we were there to *continue it.*

Ryan Matthew Landis

3

CHALLENGES

*To be tested is good.
The challenged life may be the best therapist.*

Gail Sheehy

The First Time's Always the Worst

*H*umor tells you where the trouble is.

Louise Bernikow

The first mammogram is the worst—especially when the machine catches on fire. That's what happened to me. The technician positioned me exactly as she wanted: Think of a really complicated game of Twister—right hand on the blue, left shoulder on the yellow, right breast as far away as humanly possible from the rest of your body. Then she clamped the machine down so tight, I think my breast actually turned inside out. I'm pretty sure Victoria's Secret doesn't have a bra for that.

Suddenly, there was a loud popping noise. I looked down at my right breast to make sure it hadn't exploded. Nope, it was still flat as a pancake and still attached to my body. "Oh, no," the technician said loudly. These are, perhaps, the words you least want to hear from any health professional. Suddenly, she went flying past me, lab coat whipping behind, on her way out the door. She yelled over her shoulder, "The machine's on fire! I'm going to get help!"

Okay, I was wrong. "The machine is on fire" are the worst words you can hear from a health professional, especially if you're all alone and semipermanently attached to A MACHINE and don't know if it's THE MACHINE in question.

I struggled for a few seconds to get free, but even Houdini couldn't have escaped. I decided to go to plan B: yelling at the top of my lung (the one that was still working).

I hadn't seen anything on fire, so my panic hadn't quite reached epic proportions, but then I started to smell smoke coming from behind the partition. *This is ridiculous,* I thought. *I can't die like this. What would they put in my obituary? Cause of death: breast entrapment?*

I may have inhaled some fumes because I started to hallucinate. An imaginary fireman rushed in with a fire hose and a hatchet. "Howdy, ma'am," he said. "What's happened here?" he asked, averting his eyes.

"My breasts were too hot for the machine," I quipped, as my imaginary fireman ran out of the room again. "This is gonna take the Jaws of Life!"

In reality, the technician returned with a fire extinguisher and put out the fire. She gave me a big smile and released me from the machine. "Sorry! That's the first time that's ever happened. Why don't you take a few minutes to relax before we finish up?"

I think that's what she said. I was running across the parking lot in my backless paper gown at the time. After I relaxed for a few years, I figured I might go back. But I was bringing my own fire extinguisher.

Leigh Anne Jasheway

The Hardest Mile

Success is a great healer.

Gertrude Atherton

With trembling fingers, I tie the running sneakers with a double bow as my heart races, breathing shallows and fingers fumble. One might think I was preparing for a marathon rather than one single, hopeful mile.

Slowly, I begin a stretching routine. I adjust the drawstring on my running pants, and they feel tight, a reminder of the fifteen pounds gained in as many months. I head for the door with trepidation. The brilliant rays of the sun welcome me; they caress my face and remind me of what I've been missing.

I recall my last run, eighteen months ago: It was a beautiful spring day—the kind that made me believe I could run forever. I remember vividly that I ran seven carefree miles along the rocky Atlantic coastline. I also remember the nickel-sized lump I found in my left breast while showering afterward. Mostly, I remember the panic . . . a crippling, paralyzing panic as I embarked on the hardest year of my life.

Never in my wildest dreams did I expect a diagnosis of breast cancer. Not me, not at thirty-nine years old. After all, I had always been so careful. With no family history, I still carefully checked my breasts each month. At each yearly physical examination, I waited impatiently as my doctor gave me my usual pap smear, breast exam, blood pressure check and a variety of routine blood tests. I would grin and bear the yearly mammograms and secretly scoff at each negative result. After all, I was doing all the right things. I was delighted and a little proud each time my doctor commented on my strong, slow heart rate and my clear, healthy lungs, but after all, I'd been running for years on a regular basis—five to seven miles a day, five days a week.

How could I have breast cancer?

The next few weeks were a whirlwind of tests, bone scans and surgery. Running was out of the question. Even after the wide excision lumpectomy healed, the endless weeks of radiation left me exhausted and so badly burned that running was impossible. The news that I was to undergo a long series of aggressive chemotherapy treatments was an even bigger blow. My body did not tolerate the drugs well, even the antinausea medications, and my spirit was thinner than my hair.

Now and again, on "off weeks" from the rigorous chemo schedule, I would pull on my sneakers and attempt to run a little, but each time I reluctantly gave into a walk that left me feeling even more defeated and depressed. I stopped trying. I mourned for my lost health, as well as the loss of running, which had always replenished me physically, emotionally and spiritually.

Word of my illness spread like wildfire through the small town where I live. I kept up a smiling front for all. Only my husband was aware of my growing depression. By the grace of God and the love and support of good friends and family, I made it through the darkness of that tunnel. With over a year of treatment and a barrage of clean follow-up tests behind me, I was on the road to recovery. With my doctor's okay, I began the long road back.

Bound and determined to succeed, I head up our driveway as the road welcomes me once again, and I meet it with a hesitant jog. Slowly, I head toward the old, familiar route. My breathing is labored, and beads of perspiration form on my brow; soon I feel the familiar pink flush color my face. I think how quickly I have lost my endurance and once again consider stopping, but I persevere.

Just moments into my run, I hear words of encouragement from a fellow runner, a man whose only link to me is the road we travel. "Good to see you again!" he says. "Don't give up!"

A few folks drive by and give a hearty wave and "thumbs up" sign that helps me go on. Slowly, my confidence builds, and I approach the hill that leads me home. Now I know I can do it! I have conquered bigger hills—hills that I never thought possible. At the summit I hold my head high and round the corner to catch a glimpse of my house through the trees. I smile proudly: *I did it. I ran a mile!*

It has been thirteen years since my diagnosis. I still run, counting my blessings with each step.

Jacqueline M. Hickey

One Is Enough

*Experience is not what happens to you; it's what
you do with what happens to you.*

Aldous Huxley

I was a widow and the mother of two teenagers when I
was diagnosed with breast cancer in 1973. My mother had
had a mastectomy in the 1940s, and she had gotten along
beautifully. My surgery and recovery also went well. I was
able to return to work and volunteered as the Reach to
Recovery person for our American Cancer Society.

When my first granddaughter, Heather, was about four
years old, she visited my home overnight. I had to take a
shower, so I had her stay in the bathroom with me so I
could keep an eye on her.

When I was drying off, she noticed I had only one
breast. She had lots of questions, and I tried to answer
them to her satisfaction. Finally, she hung her head in
deep thought and said, "Barney, if you have only one, why
don't you wear it in the middle?"

When I visited new mastectomy patients, I lifted a lot of
spirits with this story. God bless!

Mary Ellen "Barney" LaFavers

Blessings Beyond Belief

It's kind of fun to do the impossible.

Walt Disney

My eyes well up with tears as I watch my eight-month-old daughter, Adrianna, smile from ear to ear as she sees our reflection in the bathroom mirror. Her arms reach out to the other baby in the mirror. I still can't believe I'm holding my own daughter—I feel so blessed to have experienced the miracle of creating a new little life. She is a product of the love between my husband, Jim, and me, our miracle baby, because we weren't sure I could conceive after battling breast cancer.

Being diagnosed at age twenty-five after finding a lump in the shower was a total shock; we had only been married two years and were settling into a comfortable life, but suddenly we were researching surgery and treatment options. The biggest blow came when we discovered that chemotherapy could force a woman into menopause. I wasn't prepared for that. Breast cancer could take away my breast, but I would not let it take away my ability to have children! An oncologist told me I should not be concerned with that and instead should focus on curing my cancer. It hurt me tremendously that she didn't see how important it was to us to have a child.

Devastated, we threw ourselves into researching every option available, from postponing chemotherapy to freezing fertilized embryos. Unfortunately, there wasn't much research done on the treatment of younger women and the effects on their ability to have children. After much analysis and prayer, we decided to leave my health in the Lord's hands and go ahead with the TRAM flap surgery and six months of chemotherapy. We knew if the Lord wanted us to have children, he would provide the way—whether by natural means or adoption.

After the conclusion of my treatment, my husband and I waited several years to try to conceive, as we wanted to at least reach the five-year mark without a recurrence. Making the decision to go ahead and have children was difficult. We knew I would always be at a higher risk for the return of cancer, which in real terms meant that I might not be around to raise my children. Again, we trusted that the Lord had a plan for our family and knew we could not live in fear. After seven years, he blessed us with a precious, vibrant baby girl!

I'm so thankful for the early detection methods that were available. Because I found my lump early and didn't put off investigating it, my prognosis was great. It can be a frightening experience to get a mammogram, but as so many women can attest to, it saves lives! I not only saved my own life by following through with treatment, but as a result, I was able to give life as well. I want to encourage younger women in particular who are diagnosed with this disease to face breast cancer head on! There is so much that can be done now, and you have a lot of living left to do. Fight hard and you will come out of the experience stronger and more alive than ever!

Breast cancer has changed my life in so many unimag-inable ways. None of us choose to join the "boobie pity-party club," as I like to call it. Throughout the journey of surgeries and treatment, it is only reasonable to wonder: *Why me? Why now? Can there possibly be a purpose in all of this?*

As a newly diagnosed person, all you can do is focus on what needs to be done to heal your body. It wasn't until months later that I really looked at why this disease chose me. Now as an eight-year survivor, I can honestly say I feel breast cancer was a blessing. Yes, a blessing. After get-ting past the "why me's," I realized this health crisis in my life allowed me to take a step back, evaluate my life, and look for the meaning and truth in this experience. This struggle strengthened my faith that God had a purpose in this for my life. It is in these valleys of life that we are tested, forced to grow and are bestowed with wisdom beyond our years. I know I have traveled the cancer jour-ney so that I may be a source of encouragement and strength to other women.

I hope to empower both newly diagnosed women and survivors of many years with some of my "Cancer Reflections." Here is what I have learned:

Live life in the now. Don't always be looking ahead and miss what is happening today! Live each day as if it were your last. Death is a reality for all of us, but how you choose to live each day is up to you.

You are responsible for your own joy! Identify what makes you joyful and then seek it regularly! Life is too short to waste on things that won't last. There will always be things to complain about, but isn't it better to be opti-mistic and hopeful?

Live courageously, no matter what the circumstances. Don't let breast cancer define who you are; instead, let it affect how you embrace life. Allow God to stretch you out of your comfort zone. If you can survive breast cancer, you can take on anything!

Make God real to others, and love them without ceasing. Let others see God in you in how you speak, act, think and react to life's situations. Sometimes all we can give to another hurting person is our unconditional love.

Master your fear, or at least tame it! We all struggle with the fear of recurrence. Don't let this steal your joy. Instead, starve those fears with faith, trust and prayer.

Practice self-love. Self-love doesn't mean being selfish; it means taking care of you! Take care of your body and your emotions. Find your balance. We all need quiet time to reflect and re-energize. Don't feel guilty about not taking on yet another commitment or project. If you are a whole, healthy person, you can cope better and be an inspiration to others.

Become involved in educating about breast cancer and finding a cure! Participate in an event that raises money for breast-cancer treatment, screening or research. Call five of your best friends each month and encourage them to do their monthly breast self-exam. Join a support group to help other women through their cancer journey. I want to be an active part—however small it may be—of finding the cure! On my seventy-fifth birthday, I will celebrate fifty-years of conquering breast cancer. My grandchildren will have to be told what breast cancer was like, back in the days before there was a cure!

A fellow breast cancer friend always says, "Breast cancer only happens to the strongest of women."

Denise Blunk

The Gift of Photography
and a Beautiful Breast

*I wear the key of memory and can open every
door in the house of my life.*

Amelia E. Barr

Sometimes the things we do bring unexpected gifts. We
do these things because we're passionate to do them as
we follow our soul's desire. And by doing so, we, and
those around us, are gifted beyond measure. Photography
has given me and others such gifts.

Some time back, I was working in a wild animal rental
compound: the movie stars were great beasts like tigers,
bears and giraffes. I would see a woman trainer sitting
with a cheetah in deep-eye conversation. I would see
another trainer riding on the back of a giraffe. I saw the
owner walk across the front lawn with a Bengal tiger by
his side. I couldn't stand it any more—I went to the photo
store and bought a single-reflex camera to photograph
such beauty and wonder.

Not two weeks later, I was in the living room of the owner
and his best friend. They were two hearty and strong men,

giving each other a big bear hug. It was so beautiful I picked up my camera and photographed that hug. The best friend soon had to move from the area. I later handed the owner the photo of him and his good friend, and that image meant more to him than a pocketful of gold. That is what photography can do. Like the poet writes odes to love, photography can image an ode to an old friend.

Some time later, I was visiting my pals, Linda and Stu. They asked me if I might take some photos of them for good memories and work, and so I did. After such gorgeous images with the sun streaming behind their glistening hair, Linda asked me, "Pamela, do you mind taking some pictures of my breasts as they are now? I want to honor them; I want to honor the one that is to be leaving. I'm soon to have a mastectomy; I have cancer and feel this is the best choice."

And so we took photos of Linda's two breasts as they were, then with her holding them with her two womanly hands, and then with Stu holding them with his two manly hands, as he stood behind his wife.

And thinking about the time when photography honored Linda's breasts, and the breast that was soon to be leaving, as an ode to the beauty of what was a triumph of the spirit to honor what is gone and to celebrate what is and is yet to come—yes, that is what we all did that day together, we friends, our spirits, our bodies, the camera, the film and, most of all, the smiles in the clouds that day as they gently danced around us, reminding us we are all in this together. Some things come. Some things change form. And we can, in so many different ways, celebrate our time on this Earth together.

There are holy moments in photography. This was one of them.

Pamela Shandel

For Richer or Poorer

We didn't have a road map for this novel idea of living happily ever after, for richer or poorer, in sickness and in health. It was 1971; I was seventeen, and he was eighteen. I was still in high school, and David was barely out of high school, yet we faced the road ahead with blind faith of our undying love for each other. We each had scarce backgrounds financially and academically, but knew we had each other.

Twenty years later, my husband and I had the ideal family life: a daughter and a son, flourishing careers, and a beautiful home. How could life be any better? We felt that indeed we were on the right road to all the goodness that life had to offer—until the morning I was heading to the shower and somehow instinctively reached toward my right breast. Even though I had done breast self-exams periodically, I had never done them with concern, nor had I ever expected to find anything. This time, however, the instinctive move to my breast before I had even stepped into the shower was beyond my conscious effort, and immediately upon finding a large, hard knot, I was alarmed. Later that morning, I made an appointment with the gynecologist I had been seeing for more than twenty years.

My diagnosis was bleak. With a mastectomy forced upon me at the age of thirty-eight, so many fears controlled my thoughts that it was almost impossible to make life-saving decisions with any degree of confidence.

Our picture-perfect life had come to a screeching halt, and I went from a skilled executive-decision-maker to a woman who stumbled with not only life-saving choices, but also any simple, routine choices for daily living. Not only had I lost confidence in myself and in life, I had to try to face the realities of potential death while soothing the fears of our daughter and son. Then there was the element of intimacy with my husband. How was I supposed to make love to him in my remaining days when I didn't even know how I felt about myself as a woman? It was difficult to face the fact that someday he might want to be with another woman after my death—one who would have real breasts. These fears were almost as haunting as dying. No one discussed these issues with me, nor had I read anything on such a private matter. And it was apparent that I would have to address this soon, as my husband was showing intense interest in lovemaking before my drainage tubes were even removed. I was worried I might not ever want to make love again. And if I ever did, what type of nightgown would I wear—could I even consider not wearing a nightgown?

I continuously questioned why this experience ever happened to me, my husband, my family and our marriage. Would I ever feel that I would be feminine, desirable and alluring again?

Our first few love-making episodes after my mastectomy are ones that I will never, ever forget. I cried throughout those entire moments spent cradled in his arms. I cried for the woman I used to be. I cried for the lovemaking we used to have that would never be again. And I cried uncontrollably in the fear that my marriage would be over and David would never want me again. Yet he held me tenderly, with gentle love and quiet assurances.

It wasn't that night that I understood the depth of my husband's love; it wasn't even the weeks or months following. I still to this day reflect upon the depth of this man's love for me and marvel at what the experience of breast cancer has continued to teach me about love, and all its varying degrees, year after year since 1992.

My oncologist witnessed my husband's commitment to my healing process, as David had been at my side for every doctor's appointment since my surgery. At one follow-up appointment, however, David was not there because he had an urgent business matter to attend to. So when I went alone to the appointment, my oncologist asked me if we were still together after all David and I had been through. This question shocked me, as if the oncologist knew something that I didn't know. The oncologist then advised me that many marriages break up after breast cancer.

I reflected upon this information for days and was irate, thinking, *What is it with men!?* And, of course, I prayed that my marriage wouldn't be one of those statistics.

It took time for me to understand that it wasn't men I was really angry with for not accepting women as they were. It was me that I was deeply angry with and afraid of. I was fearful that David would see I was no longer seeing myself as a whole woman and hadn't believed in who I was even before the discovery of breast cancer.

Amazingly, life was teaching me through this journey of breast cancer that I was a whole woman with the young, beautiful breasts I used to have, as well as with the complete removal of one breast and another significantly reduced. I have learned that the more whole I feel about myself, the more whole I feel about my life and my marriage.

Without my "real" breasts, I now feel more whole as a woman than before. I never expected that the journey, which started with the words "for richer or poorer, in sickness and in health," would eventually lead me to experience richer values, in spite of my health.

Beverly Vote

"I'm past the sexy nightie stage of my life.
I've rediscovered my flannel side."

Sometimes You Just Get Lucky

If a man does his best, what else is there?

General George S. Patton

Why me? I have asked that question more times than I care to count over the past twenty-four years, and the only answer that makes any sense is "sometimes you just get lucky." I am a four-time breast-cancer survivor and have lived with cancer for most of my adult life. I know little else—I have no sense of how my life might have been without cancer. Everyone's life has a rhythm: get the kids up and off to school, hurry to work, rush to the supermarket after work to buy food for the next day's breakfast, check homework, get kids to bed on time, then collapse into bed to recharge for another day.

My life rhythm is almost identical, but it includes another element that those spared from breast cancer will never know: regular visits to the oncologist, scans, X-rays, ultrasounds, biopsies, surgeries, breast reconstruction, implants, chemotherapy, radiation, tamoxifen, reading and researching, blood tests, and more. It's a carefully choreographed movement that develops its own rhythm. Get the kids up, rush to work, visit the oncologist, get blood work done, pick up the toaster waffles, check homework, read the latest findings on a new and promising drug or vaccine, then bedtime for all.

That is my life. Most wouldn't trade theirs for mine, whatever the price, yet I consider myself lucky and wouldn't trade places with them either. I don't always catch the green lights at precisely the right moment or choose the quickest line at the supermarket. But how could I not feel lucky? I'm fifty-three years old and still here! Since my first diagnosis of breast cancer at the age of twenty-nine, I've had the privilege of waking to 8,760 mornings. I've celebrated twenty-four birthdays. I carried, delivered, nurtured and raised two beautiful children, now in their teens, who show great promise for a bright future. I played a mean game of tennis for years. I jumped for joy at the publication of my first children's book. I've learned to sail. I have a house with a view of the water. All this, while living with breast cancer. How could anyone think my life has not been lucky?

Friends and family have told me often they could NEVER go through what I've been through. This statement is a curious one. I want to ask, "Would the alternative be better?" We all know the answer to that question.

Somehow, when faced with adversity, strength pays you a visit. It invites itself in and begins its transformation on your inner being. Emotions, resolve, the will to win, all of which have been at a constant simmer, begin to boil and erupt with a determination to beat this challenging opponent. Does everyone win? Sadly, no. There are no quick and ready answers as to why. But you must try with a vengeance to ensure you'll be here to do whatever it is you're destined to accomplish. My belief in that thought kept me going through each biopsy or chemotherapy treatment. I knew my journey had miles to go, and I couldn't give up without my best effort.

People often ask me, "If you could relive your life, would you change anything, or wish to be cancer-free?"

My answer is always no. Everything that has happened to me, including having had cancer four times, has led me to this exact place in my life. There is a reason my life evolved the way it did. Someday I hope to learn that reason.

Has cancer been easy? Not always. Did it change my focus? Absolutely! Has it forced me to stop and pay attention to the important things in my life? Without question. And I wouldn't change a thing. I like a good challenge, and I'll take luck wherever I can get it.

Arlette Braman

I Am Not Alone

There are only two ways to live your life. One is as though nothing is a miracle; the other is as though everything is a miracle.

Albert Einstein

"Hi . . . am I the first?" I asked tentatively as I entered the room, and she immediately came toward me, hands outstretched in welcome.

"I'm Leatrice. Did you call me?" Her eyes were a soft, warm brown, her smile quick and sincere.

"Yes, I got the information from the hospital. I'm Janice." I nervously brushed long blonde hair over my shoulder.

"Oh, yes, Janice. Welcome. I'll be running the group tonight."

A tall Caucasian woman walked into the room, her head wrapped in a bright magenta scarf. She smiled at Leatrice, then at me.

"Hi, Joanne. This is Janice; it's her first night."

Joanne took a seat, cracked open her water bottle and had a long drink. "I'm trying to drink eight glasses a day, but it's really hard. Some days the water tastes like a metal doorknob."

"I know," Leatrice replied, her midnight black hair bobbing as she nodded her head. "Try lemonade or Gatorade. Some days it's easier to get down than water."

Two Asian women walked in. One was quite young, the other in her fifties. The older woman said, "I heard about the group from my doctor."

"Welcome. Let's begin."

Joanne raised her hand. "I'll start. I just did my second round of chemo last Thursday. I'm on A.C. for four rounds: Adriamycin and Cytoxin. I'm stage two; three lymph nodes positive. I'm having trouble with my port—it kinked up and really scared me. I was afraid they wouldn't be able to use it for the next round. The port is a godsend; it saves my veins from collapsing like my friend's did. That's why I want to keep it working perfectly. Usually I'm really happy with it."

"Are you going to drive while you go through your treatment?" Leatrice asked.

"I have to, since I can't get any time off from work."

"Be careful of the seat belt then; it can really rub on your port. I had a piece of sheepskin wrapped around the seat belt, and that really helped—kept it from rubbing," she said. "I went through breast cancer seven years ago. I had a lumpectomy, and I'm doing fine."

I looked at her in awe. She was filled with such energy, health and vitality! I marveled at the way she had graciously welcomed everyone, making each of us feel comfortable and safe. I said, "It's really inspiring to meet women who have been through this and are doing great. I look at you and begin to believe: if you can do it, I can do it."

She looked at me kindly. "Why don't you tell us about you?"

"I'm Janice, just diagnosed two weeks ago. I go in for surgery next week. I don't know yet if I need to have chemo—won't know until after the tumor and the lymph nodes are checked out. I'm having a port put in next week, and I'm really nervous about it." I looked quickly from one woman to the next. "I had a lumpectomy two weeks ago, but have to go back in for more surgery Wednesday because they didn't get clear margins the first time—the tumor was bigger than they thought it would be. They need to have a section of healthy tissue around the tumor to have a clear margin." Suddenly, all the tension and fear I'd been holding came flooding out, and I began to cry.

"I'm really confused—still in shock, I think." I struggled to talk as the tears flowed down my face. "I just can't believe this is really happening."

Leatrice pushed a box of Kleenex over to me. "It's still so new," she sighed.

Another woman spoke up. "I'll go next: I'm Sandra, twenty-eight. I was diagnosed with stage three, several tumors in each breast. I had a double mastectomy four months ago, and I'm going to have reconstruction as soon as possible. I don't know why this happened to me; I have no history of breast cancer in my family. I think you can drive yourself crazy trying to figure out why. There is no 'why.' What is, is. You just have to face it and get on with it."

Another woman said, "I'm so hot!" and she reached up and took off her baseball cap, along with the wig she wore underneath. "Whew, that's better! I can't handle this thing." Her head was covered with fine, downy fuzz about a quarter of an inch long.

"Hey! Look at that! You have hair, girl." Leatrice was laughing.

"It's starting to come back in—finally. I'm sick of this wig. I went in for my last chemo four weeks ago and have been in radiation for a week. I go every day. It takes about ten minutes, no sweat. After chemo, anything is a piece of cake, if you ask me."

"How long do you have to go for radiation?" Joanne asked.

"Thirty-three treatments, about six to seven weeks, then I'm done—I hope." She brushed her hand over her head and smiled, "It's really coming in soft. Like a baby."

I must have been staring at her because she turned to me. "The best thing is if you shave your own head. Don't wait for the disease to take your hair—do it yourself. It will make you feel much more powerful, like you're the boss, not the cancer."

"Thanks," I said.

Soon the two hours were over. I felt elated. My first breast-cancer support group had been so powerful. I'd learned about ports and wigs and clear margins. I'd seen the proud beauty and strength of these women, and I felt as though I was being heard and understood in a way that none of my friends or family could provide. Only someone who had walked the path could give me the answers I sought. After months of searching, I had found a sanctuary, a temple of wise women to guide and train me.

I was not alone.

Mary Olsen Kelly

4

CHARACTER

Character cannot be developed in ease and quiet. Only through experiences of trial and suffering can the soul be strengthened, vision cleared, ambition inspired and success achieved.

Eleanor Roosevelt

Laundry Soap

This is the first time I've sat and thought about what I really want to do, and what I really want is to be a grandmother.

Diahann Carroll

The Marie Curie Cancer Care center in North London is a hospice for the terminally ill. Surrounded by green lawns and leafy trees, it seemed more like the small community hospital in my former Maine hometown than the large, forbidding Victorian structure I was attending for my cancer treatments. The center had kindly loaned the use of what they called the library (really just a large, open room with comfortable chairs and a couple of bookcases) to a newly formed cancer support group.

I arrived early for my first meeting—nervous, frightened and unsure of exactly what it was I was doing there. I had family and friends who loved me and who were being supportive. I had never had a problem sharing my thoughts and feelings with them, but I had read that support groups increase survival rates, so there I was. I was going to be a survivor, after all.

I was greeted, welcomed, offered a cup of tea (it is England, after all), and asked who I was, where I lived, where had I heard about them. Even with tea, my mouth was dry, and I struggled to answer.

"When were you diagnosed?" asked a Skinny Woman who seemed to be about my age.

"Last month," I replied.

"When was your operation?" inquired Baldie with Big Earrings.

"Three weeks ago."

A pause. Then, gently, from the Well-Dressed Matron in the corner, "What did they find?"

"Ten nodes positive," I answered.

There was a longer pause. I was dealing with experts here, and we all knew that wasn't good. Finally, from Baldie again, "How are you doing?"

"I'm feeling very positive," I replied with practiced stoicism. "I'll do whatever is necessary to get through this. I'm sure I'm going to make it. I'm strong. I'm fairly young. I'm a fighter. I'm going to be okay." The words tumbled out, the same ones I spoke to my family, to my friends.

I looked around. Everyone smiled warmly and nodded encouragement. And none of them believed a word I said. Out of the silence, I plunged into the truth like a cold lake and came up sputtering.

"I don't understand what's happening to me. And sometimes, out of nowhere, like last night, I think the oddest stuff. I was sitting on my sofa, and I looked across my living room at my bookcase, jammed full of books and papers, and even more books and papers behind that. And the thought just popped into my head: I'd better clear that out. I sure don't want my family to have to do it after I'm dead." I came up for air.

I had admitted the unadmittable. No matter how positive I felt, no matter how strong I tried to be, someplace,

down deep, I knew I was going to die. Tears filled my eyes.
Now was the time for a little pitying sentiment, surely. I
deserved a hug or a reserved English pat on the arm, at the
very least. Why else would I open my heart to a group of
strangers with whom I had nothing in common?

Laughter and guffaws, shrieks and whoops washed
over me. Stunned, my tears disappeared as quickly as they
had formed.

"You should have been here last week," choked out
Baldie, the Journalist, through little hiccuping laughs. I
stared at these crazy people.

The matron, Rosie, the Hampstead Barrister, chipped in,
"I'd just moved back here from Singapore when I got my
diagnosis, and, of course, I didn't own a warm coat. But all
I could think was what a waste of money it would be. I
froze all that winter."

"My thing was 'travel size,'" chipped in Skinny Woman,
Linda the Art Therapist from Crouch End. "I couldn't
bring myself to buy the economy size anything, so for two
years, every time I went to the store, I bought little tiny
packs and bottles of laundry detergent and dishwashing
liquid and shampoo."

Everyone had a story more ridiculous than the last. No
one thought it odd that not only was I extremely positive
I was going to live, but also certain I was going to die. And
no one fell off her chair when I admitted it. This was my
introduction to the patient-run, unconventional support
group that was to become so important to me during my
treatment and recovery.

There were other meetings less cheerful, others even
more rowdy. Over the years, we lost members, both to
cancer and back to their healthy lives. We held Christmas
parties and birthday celebrations and memorials. But in
those weeks and months of learning to live with breast
cancer, I shared my journey with fellow travelers who

understood my illness and my fears, and taught me to laugh at both.

At the first meeting I attended after I finished my treatment, one of my new friends presented me with a gift. You know, to this day, all these years later, I don't think that I have ever seen such a large box of laundry detergent!

Lolly Susi

"I'm done with chemo . . . now I'm ready
for my hug therapy."

The Esther Bunny Lives Here

Where there is a woman, there is magic.
Ntozake Shange

For nine years my wife and I managed a small eighteen-unit oceanfront condominium complex on Maui called Hoyochi Nikko. That time often felt like the Hawaiian version of Alex Haley's Hotel. We lived in one of the units, and most of the other units were in a vacation rental program, which allowed the owners to rent their condos out by the night or the week when they weren't personally using them. We enjoyed this arrangement. We had grown to like the fact that people on vacation generally arrive in a good mood, don't stay long and are soon on their way with several rolls of film to help them relive their experience with every neighbor and relative. Often we were greeted with hugs and kisses from new guests sent by previous guests who had long ago faded from our memory. But this story is about the one who didn't leave—the Esther Bunny.

In 1998, a young man who frequently surfed in front of

our place asked if he could see one of the condos that had recently come up for sale. My wife, Micki, politely showed him the unit, wondering how his lifestyle would fit in with the vacationers who normally occupied the complex. After looking, he said, "I think my mother would like living here; I'll bring her by after she heals from her hip surgery."

When Micki passed along the story to me, we discussed how we might handle the situation if an older person in need of care became a permanent resident. All the scenarios we came up with sounded like they wouldn't work. We soon dropped the subject and expected that anyone in that situation would also come to the same conclusion.

A few months went by, and the young man stopped by again and said his mother was ready to look at the property. The original unit had sold, but we knew of another that might be for sale. We made the arrangements, and a few days later he showed up with his mother. To my surprise, she didn't appear to have recovered from her surgery—her son kept a chair in hand and several times during the showing he gently slid it under his mother. She seemed to quickly recharge her batteries while sitting and would rise for another five minutes, exclaiming, "This is beautiful!" That was our first introduction to Esther.

The rest of the day and most of the next we worried that Esther was going to be a part of our day-to-day routine. As fate would have it, she bought the condo and moved in by herself. I was terrified that this small, fragile lady wouldn't be able to take care of herself or might get injured and I would be responsible. In truth, I was more worried about me than Esther.

She would never be known as a quick mover, but she healed, and our concerns about her faded. We found that, short of skydiving, she answered, "Count me in," to anything we suggested.

Within a short time we found that we looked to Esther

as a place to get our own emotional batteries charged. She started joining us for frequent movie nights at home, going to the theater, shopping and dining out. Soon she became my Esther Bunny. If anyone was a bother, it was probably me. I found myself stopping by frequently to say "Hi," not because I was worried, but because I enjoyed her company. Her ability to keep a positive attitude, to smile and laugh easily, caused me to frequently try and analyze her, wanting to add Esther-like qualities to my own life. I noticed that vacationers and part-time residents were quick to include her in their activities, too, not because they felt sorry for her, but because she added so much to their lives.

A few years later, Esther's other hip went bad. She found it difficult to get up from a chair and extremely painful to walk. She said, "At eighty-seven, I'm too old to go through another surgery."

Micki told her, "We expect you to be around until you're at least a hundred, and you might as well be able to walk without pain." I told her that Hoyochi Nikko was getting a basketball team together and that she wouldn't be able to be on the team unless she got the hip replaced. I think it was Micki's logic that prevailed, but I enjoyed kibitzing with her over the other possible reasons she might want to endure the process.

Recovery wasn't fast, but she made it and kept all of us in good spirits while she once again went through hip replacement.

Recently, Esther was diagnosed with breast cancer. She had her lymph nodes removed and was given the option of doing radiation or not receiving treatment. We asked people who had gone through the process, as well as those in the medical profession, what they recommended. We were told that cancer normally moves slowly in older people, and the radiation can be painful and stressful. With this knowledge in hand, she made the decision to proceed with the treatment.

Hoyochi Nikko isn't known to have a basketball team, but word has spread of our resident Esther Bunny. I think Esther has decided that she will squeeze everything out of life that comes her way. I don't see her as an older person, but as someone who has chosen to incorporate positive influences in her life and let the weight of negatives fall by the wayside. That little old lady I feared would affect my life did.

Ron Lando-Brown

Crooked Wigs and Guinea Pigs

The steamy August afternoon in the summer of 1996 was just about more than I could take. Sitting in my car at a red light, I was nauseated from my recent chemotherapy treatment, in pain from other cancer medications and severely depressed from the whole cancer experience. I was also at the end of my patience with my husband, who had, just that morning, encouraged me yet again to smile and to try to have a more positive attitude and a sense of humor.

Roger knew what he was talking about. You see, he was fighting his own battle with cancer. Unbelievably, at the relatively young age of forty-five, we had *both* been diagnosed with cancer within six weeks of one another—I with breast cancer with positive lymph nodes, and he with what one doctor described as a "particularly nasty" form of kidney cancer. Roger somehow managed to be upbeat and hopeful through it all. That I could not seem to find my way to the same state of mind only added to my frustration and depression.

And the sticky mid-Atlantic heat and humidity just made everything worse. All I wanted was to finish my errands, go home and crawl into bed.

Noticing that my wig felt lopsided, I took advantage of the red light to look into the rearview mirror. I tugged on the sides and front of the wig to straighten it and saw, to my horror and embarrassment, four teenagers in the car behind me mocking my movements! They were modeling in exaggerated fashion the primping of a vain woman posing before a mirror, and they were laughing themselves silly.

Tears of anguish welled up in my eyes. *How could they be so cruel?* I wondered. *How could they make fun of a sick woman, a woman who might even be dying?*

Because they don't know, I quickly answered myself. *And besides, they're just kids. They don't know any better.*

Then I thought, *But they should.*

I don't know where it came from—maybe I was delirious from the heat—but a giggle bubbled up inside me and, without another thought, I placed my right hand on top of my head and yanked off my wig. Still looking in the mirror, I gave a huge shrug of my shoulders and laughed out loud just as the light turned green.

I will never forget the look of total shock on those four teenagers' faces as I pulled away from the intersection. All four had their hands to their cheeks, and their mouths and eyes were as big and round as dinner plates. I can still hear the horns of other cars blaring at them to move as they sat there, stunned and motionless.

I laughed for three days. And, for the most part, I haven't stopped laughing since, because what I discovered that day was that the physical act of laughing made me feel physically better.

Now a lot of people—including Roger—had been telling me for a long time that "laughing will make you feel better," but I thought they meant on some higher, esoteric level, and my head and heart just weren't in the mood for that.

What I hadn't understood was that laughing would

make me feel physically better. And that, in fact, laughing would make me physically healthier.

Once I made myself laugh by removing my wig to shock those young people, I realized I could make myself laugh pretty much anytime I wanted to.

And that's when I started getting well.

Since then, I've learned that laughter improves your cardiovascular system in much the same way as aerobic exercise. It oxygenates your entire body, and there is some evidence that it lowers your blood pressure and releases endorphins (the "feel good" chemicals) in your brain. Physical discomforts are minimized almost immediately and—even better—your immune system is strengthened. Not only is your body better able to withstand the rigors of any medical treatment you might be undergoing, but it is also better able to fight disease on its own in the ways God and nature intended. *Every single time you laugh, you become physically healthier, and you ensure that you will be even healthier tomorrow!*

Do whatever you have to do to make yourself laugh. One tried-and-true method is to watch funny movies (go to *www.afi.com*, click on "Quick Links" and then "100 Years ... 100 Laughs" for the American Film Institute's list of the 100 funniest movies ever made; then start working your way through the list) and television shows like *America's Funniest Home Videos*. I have laughed myself stupid over some of those videos, especially the ones of babies trying new foods or ones showing the antics of dogs and cats.

Give a kitten a piece of ribbon. Read a book by Erma Bombeck or Dave Barry or another humorous author. Blow bubbles and watch a toddler try to catch them. Ask a six-year-old what the president's job is. Listen to comedy tapes and CDs—your local music store has a whole section devoted to humor. There are countless ways to make yourself laugh.

Shortly after my diagnosis, my doctor offered me the opportunity to participate in a clinical trial, and I eagerly accepted. He didn't use the term "guinea pig," but that's how I saw myself. It didn't matter, though. I wanted every available weapon to fight my battle!

The actual treatments using the trial drug began many months later. The drug was brutal, but by then I had learned the healing power of laughter. While browsing in one of those everything-costs-a-dollar stores, looking for something to amuse myself, I found a small face mask that was just a rubber nose with whiskers. It looked like a mouse's nose. *Or maybe a rat's. Or maybe,* I thought, *a guinea pig's.*

At my next appointment, I sat on the table in the examining room sporting my shiny bald head, that oh-so-lovely hospital gown, my new nose and whiskers, and a terribly serious expression. When my doctor walked in, he asked (head down and looking at my chart), "And how are we today?"

I said in the saddest voice I could muster, "I don't know about this clinical trial. I'm starting to feel like a guinea pig."

He looked up at me with a puzzled expression. A smile spread slowly across his face. Then he chuckled. Then he started laughing. He laughed so hard he had to sit down. I laughed so much my sides hurt and tears rolled down my face. That rubber nose was the best dollar I ever spent.

Whether you spend a dime or a dollar or nothing at all, find a way to laugh every day. It truly is an investment in your health.

Kathy Cawthon

Sixty Miles

I suppose if I had to choose just one quality to have, that would be it: vitality.

John F. Kennedy

When I first signed up for a sixty-mile walk to raise money for breast-cancer research, I was most excited about the personal challenge of walking twenty miles a day, sleeping in a tent and surviving three days without the comforts of home. I had been working to get in shape, and the breast-cancer walk gave me the opportunity to reach a demanding fitness goal while doing some good at the same time. It turned out to be so much more.

The first day of the event, 4,800 walkers gathered bright and early at a convention center, ready for the experience of a lifetime. Volunteers collected our luggage and sleeping bags, and told us we could retrieve them at base camp. Opening ceremonies began with walkers forming an enormous, three-layered semicircle. The first layer was open space, symbolizing the spirits of the people lost to breast cancer. The second layer was for cancer survivors. It was packed full of people in pink T-shirts, some still bald from treatment, realizing they were not alone in their fight. The outer layer, where I stood, was for people supporting the cure who had never battled cancer themselves.

We listened as speakers shared statistics and words of encouragement, and we learned, according to the American Cancer Society, that more than 182,000 women in the United States would be diagnosed with breast cancer over the next year and more than 40,000 would die. Early detection is key, as the five-year survival rate for people treated in the early stages of breast cancer is 96 percent.

Determined to save lives, our group raised more than $6,750,000 to be spent on improving access to care for underserved women and advancing cancer research. It was awe-inspiring to realize what the combined efforts of many could accomplish. After the presentations, we held hands and devoted a long moment of silence to remembering loved ones lost to breast cancer.

Motivated that we would be making a difference with every step, it was time to start our sixty-mile journey. A sea of walkers took over the roads. Volunteer motorcycle clubs helped control traffic. I'll never forget one big, tough rider dressed in black leather, his Harley adorned with pink ribbons in honor of his wife.

I walked and walked, cried and walked. My tears flowed as I read people's T-shirts. Many listed people in a community or church fighting cancer. Most focused on one special person, like the jerseys worn by three sisters in honor of the sister they had lost. A lot of participants had pictures of the person for whom they walked pinned to the back of their shirt. The pictures hit me the hardest, as I was forced to visualize the actual people behind the statistics. The photo that upset me the most was of a beautiful, vibrant college co-ed with a bright smile. Her picture was ironed onto the shirts of her sorority sisters, who were walking in her memory. She was only twenty-four years old when she died from breast cancer.

We treaded through poverty-stricken neighborhoods, ritzy suburbs, historic towns and city streets. I was privileged to hear so many personal stories over the miles, both tragic and inspirational. The heaviness of the journey was lightened by the huge number of survivors participating and by the great volunteers who gave us food and water at each pit stop while cheering: "2-4-6-8, hydrate! Stretch! Urinate!"

After twenty miles we arrived at our base camp on the athletic fields of a middle school. I will not lie: my feet were swollen and in pain, and I questioned if I could do this for two more days. Limping, I set up my tent and realized I was not alone. People hobbled all around me, some on crutches, some with moleskin all over their feet, some with wrapped-up knees. Then it hit. This was nothing compared to dealing with breast cancer. We all vowed to somehow get up and do it again tomorrow.

The first night was cold, and I wasn't the most prepared camper in the group. Luckily, exhaustion allowed me to fall asleep easily. I won't mention the details of having to use a port-a-potty at four A.M. in complete darkness, but trust me . . . I longed for indoor plumbing.

The next two days my feet blistered and my muscles ached, but the harmonious goodwill and group spirit kept me going. I met phenomenal people and was blessed to be among a mass of human kindness for seventy-two hours. By the end, the sixty miles had nothing to do with a fitness goal. It was about the cause, the memory of those who had lost their lives to breast cancer and all the innumerable survivors. Crossing our finish line felt like a triumph for all!

Sherrie Page Najarian

Angels

Angels are pure thoughts from God, winged with Truth and Love.

Mary Baker Eddy

My breast cancer was found during a routine mammogram, and diagnosis and surgery were done all within a two-week time frame. I had a left breast mastectomy, seventeen nodes removed, and chemotherapy to follow later.

My breast cancer journey could be a book in itself. The love and support of my husband, family and friends were overwhelming—cards, letters and gifts started to arrive, with one single theme in common: angels. I have always believed in the presence of angels and asked for their help many times, mostly to watch over my two children, especially when they were teenage drivers. I never failed to ask their guardian angels to please bring them home safely each night.

The angels started coming—angels for my car, angel worry rocks, angel pins and every card had an angel on it, all of which I treasured. But not long after my chemotherapy treatments were over, I had sort of a "let down." I thought, *Everything that can be done has been done . . . so now what?* I wanted to truly live.

I decided after this life-altering journey to do something wild and crazy. I had already decided against reconstructive surgery, so I planned to have a tattoo! Before breast cancer, I wouldn't have dreamed of doing such a thing, but I didn't know my future and I was going for it!

I felt it was appropriate to get an angel tattoo on my right shoulder—a permanent "angel watching over me." I had the tattoo artist add a small teardrop falling from her left eye to signify that I would never be the same. Amazingly, the teardrop disappeared after a few months! I know sometimes the ink fades over time, but I choose to believe this was a sign from God and the angels that I was going to be okay. And I just celebrated my anniversary of five years cancer-free!

Pamela Pierce

From Stressed to Blessed

Art washes away from the world the dust of everyday life.

Pablo Picasso

There isn't a day that goes by in which "doodling" hasn't helped me meet any new challenge that comes my way. Sound a bit crazy? Believe me, I was the first person who thought I must have lost my mind to think that something that sounds so frivolous and meaningless could become such a powerful learning tool. But it did! And now I travel across the United States and to other countries teaching people of all ages how they can reduce stress and develop more trust in the unpredictable, yet creative adventure called life.

It all began in 1995 when I was first diagnosed with breast cancer, then continued in 1997 when I was, once again, diagnosed with cancer in my other breast. One day, while nervously waiting for test results at my doctor's office, I found myself fidgeting with all the magazines, trying to focus on the words. After scanning through at least ten publications, I realized nothing was helping me relax and stay calm. My mind was beginning to run wild, imagining all sorts of worrisome scenarios. *What if this happens? What if that happens?* I'm sure if the nurse had taken my vital signs at that moment they would not have been considered "within normal limits."

I knew I needed to do something, so I asked the nurse for a piece of paper and pen. I returned to my seat and began to doodle. I had no idea what I was creating as I let the pen freely wander on the paper, yet out of nowhere abstract art seemed to materialize. I decided to have some fun and create one guideline: to begin and end the doodle outline at the same point in one continuous movement, without lifting the pen off the paper—and do it quickly. Who knows where that idea came from? I was beginning to have a lot of fun while I waited for the doctor. Then an amazing thing happened: while lost in this creative activity, I began to experience a sense of calm and peace. I noticed my preoccupation with negative thoughts subside.

I knew I had stumbled onto something quite powerful, although I had yet to put all the pieces together. All I knew was that doodling helped bring me back to a more centered and peaceful space in the midst of a frightening and challenging medical situation.

I continued to doodle after that day and bought a special spiral notebook that became my doodle book. I took it everywhere (the carwash, hairdresser, meetings), especially when I knew I'd be waiting. I even kept the doodle book with me as I lay on a gurney in the operating room before surgery. It became my constant companion—especially when waiting for daily radiation therapy at the hospital. I loved to doodle so much that I would even show up at the hospital early just to get in more doodle time.

After a while, others began to take notice and admire some of the art I created. As each doubted their own ability, I'd put the pen and a blank piece of paper in their hand and say, "Now it's your turn to create your own doodle!" The next day we all had something new to share with one another, and this simple, pleasurable activity became a powerful ice-breaker, opening up lines of communication, which for some led to personal friendships that continue to this day.

As time went on, I decided to put all my doodles into a book as a way to honor this newfound magical world that somehow totally transformed my adventure through breast cancer. *But what did I know about publishing a book?* I wondered. I had no background in the publishing world. Then I stopped and thought about what the doodles had actually taught me. The pieces started to come together ... one of those "light-bulb" moments. You see, I also spent many years studying and practicing meditation and Eastern philosophy, and the one teaching that kept bubbling to the surface time and time again—doodle after doodle—was the teaching of how powerful the present moment is—that NOW space in time. I also began to appreciate how all those scary what-if scenarios were nothing more than a projection into the unknown future. When I looked at this form of doodling, I began to appreciate that beautiful art had been created by simply letting go of control and having more faith and trust in the process itself—that journey between the beginning and end. And when I connected with that space in the middle, I also discovered inner strength, courage, wisdom and peace.

Wow! What a major breakthrough that had been for me. I thought, *If I can trust in the present moment and create amazing art without knowing the outcome ahead of time, then I should be able to take that same understanding and apply it to my life, especially my journey through a medical crisis.* And it was true! That has been one of the most powerful gifts that came to me through breast cancer, and I continue to take that understanding to whatever challenge that knocks on my door. From the unexpected flat tire to dealing with elderly parent issues, doodling remains a constant and steady companion, reminding me that life is all about the journey and the choices we make along the way. Yes, it's filled with many unexpected twists and turns, yet each can provide us with an opportunity to discover the greatness of who we truly are.

Carol Ross Edmonston

Becoming a Transformed Woman

Believe in something larger than yourself.

Barbara Bush

I was diagnosed with breast cancer in 1992 at age thirty-eight. I underwent transformation surgery in July 1992. That's what my husband Al called it, and it is the term I have since adopted. I use that phrase when I am with patients, whom I have the privilege to help at the Johns Hopkins Breast Center.

Al told me, "The surgeon's mission is to transform you from a victim into a breast-cancer survivor. You are exchanging your breast for another chance at life, and that is a fair trade." Though disappointed I wasn't a candidate for reconstruction, our daughter, Laura, age twelve, set me straight and wrote the following poem:

Appearance

Nobody's perfect
Just look at me
But if you really think about it

Who wants to be.
Beauty and glamour
Are nice to get
But it's what's inside that counts
You must never forget.
I hope you understand
What I've been trying to say
I hope you get well soon
And I love you more each day.
                                        Love, Laura

Six weeks after surgery I was fitted for my breast prosthesis. I selected a name for her—"Betty Boob." My silhou-
ette was whole again, and I stood tall once more, all five
feet, two inches of me. I was growing more confident week
by week, and month by month, about my appearance and
sexual being.

At age forty, I had another bad mammogram. Betty Boob
got a roommate, Bobbie Sue. To validate my womanhood
and my husband's love for me, he took me away to the
Pocono Mountains (where the honeymooners go) for a long
weekend. He said, "I've read before when you lose one of
your senses, like your sense of sight or sense of smell, your
other senses become more intensified. Maybe the same
thing happens to your erotic zones. I intend to prove this
hypothesis in the next forty-eight hours." He did.

In 2002, the opportunity to have DIEP flap reconstruction became an option for me, and I pursued it—first with
hesitation, then with enthusiasm. I didn't have the choice
in 1992 or 1994 to do reconstruction with my mastectomy
surgeries.

My brain went into overdrive. *Was it okay for me to pursue
this? Did I deserve this opportunity? Am I being selfish?* I prayed
about it. I was leaving church one evening and asked God
to please give me a sign that it was okay to proceed with

the reconstruction surgery. In my car as the engine started, the car radio played the song "Sexual Healing." The first full verse I heard was, "You're my medicine, come on and let me in. I can't wait for you to operate." It was the sign I needed, rational or not!

As I showered the morning of my surgery, I rubbed the bar of soap across my chest for the last time. I had always said when I looked down in the shower, I didn't see my breasts were gone—I saw the cancer was gone. I realized that soon I would be seeing two healthy, surgically created breasts that would be cancer-free and remain that way for life, hopefully. Surgery was performed in December 2002. Once asleep, I knew my hospital gown would be lifted up to my neck, exposing my body. I prepared typed signs to wear, which were taped to my chest and abdomen—some comic relief for the OR staff. Over my right mastectomy incision, it said: "Please super-size me." Over my left mastectomy incision, it said: "I'm here for a front-end realignment." And over my navel, it said: "Dear Santa, thanks for bringing me cleavage for Christmas." The signage brought a laugh to the OR team, as intended. I also realized this would be yet another form of transformation surgery.

The day my drains came out and I was able to get in the shower without tubes and devices in my way, I took a bar of soap and slowly washed my new breasts with tears streaming down my face. It was a profound moment. The "girls" and I were home and doing fine (and they were each capable of holding a bar of soap under their mammary fold).

At five weeks post-op, my husband and I quickly turned into a pair of honeymooners, test-driving my new body often. He told his brother, "I feel like I'm sleeping with another woman and have my wife's permission."

Our daughter took me bra shopping—an event that

should have been videotaped: three hours of laughter and twice a few tears. She went through the department-store bras and proceeded to show me what a bra can do for a woman's breasts today: lift them up, push them together, pull them apart, add a cup size and deepen cleavage. You name it, and there's a bra that can do it. Now I'd be wearing bras that had names, color and designer configurations that really should come with an operator's manual.

I still smile with joy in the shower every morning when the girls and I get wet and soapy. And perhaps I'm even more pleased than most women would be because I have mourned the loss of my breasts, was resolved I would never have them again and was given the gift of choice at long last—to choose or not to choose reconstruction. Was it worth the wait? You betcha!

What did I do with Betty Boob and Bobbie Sue, my breast prostheses? I wanted to select someone very special to receive them. They are happily resting on the chest of an underserved woman whom I have had the privilege to take care of at the Johns Hopkins Breast Center. Once fitted in my mastectomy bras, with Betty Boob and Bobbie Sue tucked inside, she hugged me tight for giving her this special gift of an important piece of me from an important time in my life: my bosom buddies. I realized at that moment, as we were embracing, that my new breasts were actually hugging my old prosthetic breasts. It was as if my old girls perhaps were saying, "Welcome to Lillie's. We know you will enjoy your stay. We did. She's full of life and love and energy like no one else we know. You will meet many newly diagnosed women with breast cancer just as we have over the last decade. She will utilize you as she did us—giving women hope and reminding them this is a disease that is emotionally charged and tests our psyches. We'll come by to visit periodically with our new owner. Again, welcome."

Lillie Shockney, R.N., B.S., M.A.S.

The Graduation

I personally measure success in terms of the contribution an individual makes to her or his fellow human beings.

Margaret Mead

I patiently waited for the phone to ring. It was 5:10 on Friday afternoon, December twenty-ninth, and I still hadn't heard from Mom. This was the big day . . . day thirty-five . . . the final radiation treatment for her breast cancer. I knew she would have had her last radiation jolt at 3:30 P.M., her daily treatment time since the middle of November.

Yesterday, our whole family met to have lunch and see a movie to celebrate the end of her treatments. During lunch, family members kept making kidding comments. "Raise your hand if you used Mom's cancer as an excuse to get out of something these past few months." More than half of us raised our hands.

"Be nice!" Mom joked. "I've got cancer!"

"It's gone now, Mom," we chimed in.

At the end of our special day, we gathered around her

car. It had taken us twenty minutes in the underground parking cavern to find the lavender pole marked C7 where she thought she was parked. My mother always gets lost in parking structures.

As I helped her into the car, I handed her a tiny gold-wrapped package. "Here, Mom, this is for you," I said. My emotions cut loose and embarrassed me as the tears poured down my cheeks.

"You're crying, Heather," Mom said in a soft, motherly tone.

"Shhh," I said, turning around to see if anyone in the family was watching, and I caught my sister's eye. She knew I'd hidden the little "graduation gift" in my purse all afternoon. I was waiting for the right time to give it to her. "It's all right," my sister mouthed to me.

I turned back to Mom. "Please don't open this gift until tomorrow, AFTER your last radiation."

On the way home, I told my children why I got so emotional when I gave Nana her gift. It was not out of sadness, but my reaction to Mom's incredible humor and positive outlook during her entire experience with what she calls the "Big C." She never felt sorry for herself, never blamed anyone and never complained . . . ever.

Throughout her ordeal, she brought her unique sparkle into the lives of other cancer patients and the hospital staff. Daily, she'd call and tell me about the people she had seen at the center. There was a seventy-ish wealthy attorney battling prostate cancer, married to a twenty-something woman; he always sits next to Mom in the treatment waiting area. His doting wife is attentive, but clearly has a lot on her hands with him. One day, he poked his head out of the dressing-room door before he changed into his hospital gown. He asked my mother to join him after he closed the door so that they "could fool around." The other patients roared with laughter. I'm not so sure the wife did.

And then there was the thirty-one-year-old, grossly overweight man with a large brain tumor. His father brought him to the center every day for his radiation. Mom's new friend chose to wait in the hallway outside the designated waiting room; she thinks it's because he's self-conscious about his appearance. "It's not just the weight," she told me. "His facial features are slightly askew, too." When she passed him in the hall, she always touched him and asked how he was doing. The other day, the man's father told Mom that her touch each day gives his son hope. "No one but you ever touches him," he said.

By the end of the first week of her radiation, Mom knew the name, age and astrological sign of the entire radiation staff. Just before the holidays, she brought See's candy for everyone and sent two large flower arrangements to the nurses at her surgeon's office.

During the last two weeks of her treatment, Mom got a double dose of radiation each day. I could tell she was very tired and that her skin itched terribly . . . still, no complaints.

When she was switched to the double dose, she saw the technician use a small metal piece marked "M. MacDougall," and asked if she could keep it as a souvenir. That's when I got the idea for her gift. I bought a gold calendar pendant that I had engraved "December" with the twenty-ninth crossed off. I chose a twenty-inch gold chain so the pendant would rest on her chest.

At 5:20 P.M., just as the sun was setting over the Santa Barbara mountains, the phone rang.

"Guess what!" Mom shouted on the other end. "I got a diploma! My first real diploma! It says: 'Successfully completed radiation treatment at Cedars Sinai Cancer Center,' and I never even graduated from college!"

"Mom, you're amazing!" I said, smiling into the phone.

Heather Haldeman

Chockwut Pudding

All the animals, excepting man, know that the principal business of life is to enjoy it.

Samuel Butler

I had always respected rules, did all my homework and cleaned my plate before I could have dessert. An evening with my nieces Kristi and Kelli changed all that.

The girls wanted to play "waitress" and asked me to join them. Kristi (age three) and I were seated on the couch, ready to watch "the show," and Kelli (age five) was our hostess and waitress.

"Good evening," Kelli smiled at me. "Welcome to our show. Are you ready to order?"

"Yes. I'll have popcorn with the show," I answered.

"I'm sorry, there is no popcorn. This is a *dinner* show. We are serving dinner."

"Oh, okay." I hastily adjusted my order. "I'll have a turkey sandwich."

"Very good," Kelli nodded briskly. Then she turned, peering over her imaginary order pad, to her next patron.

"What would you like to order for dinner with your show?" asked Kelli.

"Chockwut pudding," smiled Kristi.

"I'm sorry," answered the waitress. "This is a *dinner* show. We are serving *dinner*. You have to order *dinner*. Do you understand?"

Kristi nodded solemnly.

"Okay, good. So what would you like to order?" Kelli asked crisply.

"Chockwut pudding," said Kristi.

"No, Kristi! I told you—this is dinnertime. Only *dinner* is being ordered now. Afterwards, maybe you can have dessert, but this is just for dinner. So what do you want to order for *dinner*?"

"Chockwut pudding!" Kristi stated with conviction.

"You *can't* have chocolate pudding. You have to order dinner. What will you have?"

"*Chockwut pudding.*" Kristi spoke slowly and patiently, as if speaking to someone from another planet.

"Oh. *All right.*" Kelli, the perfect waitress, stomped off to serve dinner (and chocolate pudding) and start the show.

This little scenario between two adorable little girls changed the way I think about a lot of things. Why do you have to eat a big dinner to have dessert? And what if dessert is all you really want? Why is it that people who really know what they want always seem to get it? Look at how persistence really pays off if you stick to your guns. Why do we give away our power to those feeding us? And why *can't* we have chocolate pudding whenever we want it?

So now I think of "chockwut pudding" whenever something seems to be standing in my way—and I breeze right past the obstacles . . . like cancer. I think "chockwut pudding" whenever anyone implies that my goal can't be achieved, my dream can't come true, or that cancer can't be defeated. All the research, the medical technology, chemotherapy and radiation are there to keep my dreams alive . . . and they're working.

The next time someone tells you that you can't beat the odds or change your life, look them squarely in the eye and say with a smile: "Chockwut pudding!"

Mary Olsen Kelly

Spirit Undaunted!

Forget mistakes. Forget failures. Forget everything except what you're going to do now and do it. Today is your lucky day.

Will Durant

I identify myself as a swimmer and a painter these days—two things I had put off, both out of my comfort zone—before breast cancer two years ago at age sixty-three. Once the mastectomy, chemo and radiation were over, new thoughts and ideas kept popping up. I wondered, *How would swimming feel? How would it feel to put paint on a canvas and see what shows up?* The answer is: They feel great! Now I swim fifteen laps three times per week—my goal is twenty—and our living- and dining-room walls are covered with my paintings, and I love looking at them.

Nothing is the same after breast cancer . . . including my sense of humor. The other day I left my swimsuit prosthesis behind in the dressing room at the pool, and my husband Tony went to the pool to retrieve it. He told the clerk at the desk, "I need to talk to you about something embarrassing."

She took him aside and said, "That's not embarrassing. We even had a person leave a LEG here one time."

She asked someone to look for the missing swim boob in the dressing room, resorting to sign language because the woman kept saying: "What? What?" She was unfamiliar with something as complicated as a prosthesis, and English was not her native language. She found it, though, and came out of the dressing room holding it aloft by one corner with an amazed expression on her face.

I discovered it's difficult to swim and laugh at the same time.

Breast is gone, sense of humor intact, spirit undaunted, and priorities turned sideways!

Sue Caruso

Women Who Bare Their Breasts

I sing the body electric.

Walt Whitman

I am a member of a secret society of women that has no name, never meets in public and performs a ritual that would get us arrested on any street corner in America: we take our clothes off and stare at each other's bodies.

An elderly woman first invited me into this strange-seeming group at my church. In the bathroom one Sunday, she offered to let me see the flat chest that resulted from her double mastectomy. I had just been told that I had to have a mastectomy, and the image of losing a body part was haunting my days and nights. Yet here this kindly woman stood, offering this intimate reassurance. I said yes. She unbuttoned her blouse, took off her lacy bra and showed me the strong, hard lines of her little boy's chest. I thought she was beautiful, and I thought her generosity was overwhelming.

During the three weeks that followed, I had two similar offers and found that I was no longer shocked. A nurse at a doctor's office offered to let me see her rebuilt breasts. She led me into an examining room and showed me how perky silicone implants can make your breasts. Another young woman called me on the phone and invited me—a person connected to her only through the accident of our having the same surgeon—to her one-bedroom apartment by the beach to see what a Tram-flap reconstruction looked like. She was tall, with red ringlet hair, and her breast looked so real that before I even knew what I was doing, I blurted out, "Can I touch it?" She was as unfazed by the request as she was by standing in front of me half naked.

Influenced in large part by what I saw and touched that day, I chose the same surgery and became part of the secret society that had reached out, welcomed me and educated me. I have the choice to keep my mouth closed and my blouse buttoned, but for what I might gain in privacy or discretion, I would lose in the chance to see women turn from ashen-faced strangers into friends, who feel the hope that only seeing a survivor in the flesh can bring. I'm now four years past my own reconstructive surgery, and I've shown countless women my breasts. I invite them into my home; I take them into the bathroom at school; I once showed a woman my breast in the Port-a-Potty at my husband's company picnic—and she went to get the same surgery I did.

Not long ago, I was asked to show my breast on a national TV show and for a national woman's magazine because I wrote a book about breast cancer with a chapter titled "Modesty Is Irrelevant," and editors suspected I'd be willing. My initial reaction to these invitations was, "No way." This public grandstanding seemed to be a violation of the rules and the spirit of the secret society of women who bare their breasts. But the red-haired woman who showed me her breast had died from her cancer, and here

I could do for millions of women in one fell swoop the same thing she had done for me in one afternoon by the beach. It seemed a fitting tribute. So with cameras humming, I took off my clothes, smiled and said, See, here's the scar. See, this is fake. See, I am alive!

I was proud to show off my rebuilt breasts, to show off my scars, to let other women see what it means to be alive and changed. It may be a strange-sounding ritual to people outside the tribe, but to those of us inside, it's something we hold sacred.

Jennie Nash

Things Are Looking Up!

My radiation treatment itself was relatively short and painless, but lying still and getting set up on the table while technicians sight in the tattoos marking my radiation site was boring. As I lay immobilized on the table, all I could see was a huge machine above me, and my peripheral vision picked up trays of human masks for brain-tumor radiation and ominous-looking wires and equipment. The ceiling had acoustic drop-in panels with lots of holes. I had thoughts of lying there every day for six weeks counting holes in the ceiling while the crossed red laser beams gleamed above as I listened to the groan of the machinery. This was going to be a mental endurance contest.

The second day of treatment, I noticed a few ceiling tiles resting on the side wall of the room. I asked the assistant, "What is being planned for those?"

He said, "They're being replaced."

Out of the blue, I asked, "Could I take two tiles home with me and stencil designs on them?" *Wow*, I thought. *I'll need to think of a design, paint it, and then I'd have something to look at while the machine hums.*

The technician said, "Go ahead."

The first panel I brought back was well-received and

instantly installed. I chose to paint a cat among geranium pots looking out a window with stars in the sky. The staff got a kick out of it, and just having something to look at took my mind off the machine and its work. At the end of my session, I took another panel home. By the end of my treatments, I had stenciled scenes in every direction, so no matter what therapy anyone was receiving, the patient could focus on some fish on a reef, grapevines and baskets, horses galloping across a field, etc.

Needless to say, I became the talk of the treatment center during my six weeks. Elderly patients actually waited to see my next installment and thanked me for my efforts. I was able to open conversations with strangers in the waiting room. Other patients told me their fears and concerns, and I was able to alert the staff to handle their questions. I think this simple gesture made a huge difference in the center—it relaxed the patients, made the place friendlier, and warmed the hearts of all of us going through such scary and trying times.

I ultimately ended up doing a second treatment room in the same building, and word spread to my chemotherapy office, where I painted more. I even ended up traveling to Pittsburgh to work with a film crew, documenting breast-cancer survivors and their stories: *Two Chicks, Two Bikes, One Cause.*

In all, the experience lightened my heart and gave me hope for the future. Each day, I had homework, and it was fun to "think of a scene" and surprise the staff and patients in the morning. Through my small gesture, I feel I helped distract and comfort other patients. I'm so glad I found the energy to contribute to others in trying times. It did wonders for me!

Teri Reath D'Ignazio

Divine Inspiration

There are two ways of spreading light: to be the candle or the mirror that reflects it.

Edith Wharton

I really wanted my last treatment to be special for my radiation team, because they were awesome, and for myself to celebrate thirty-three days . . . thirty-three treatments.

So I decided to bake biscotti. I stayed up until 1:30 A.M., then got up early to package it, wrap it and write out cards. But something was missing. I wanted to be able to convey to the amazing people at the hospital how much I appreciated them, their professionalism and their caring dedication, and how comforting it was to have them there during my treatments.

I also wanted my gift to be something memorable, something that would brighten their day and bring smiles to their faces every time they thought of me—and make me smile every time I thought of them. (The irreverent part of me just had to have the last word!)

All of a sudden, it came to me. It was inspired—it was

brilliant—it was too stinking funny! I needed some help, though, and my husband John had already left for work, so I called a friend and asked if she would come over.

When I arrived at the hospital, I changed and went into the treatment room. For thirty-three days, the technicians had carefully positioned me and lined me up with precision according to the tattoos and marks painted on my chest to make sure they treated the correct areas.

The technician came over to position me, adjusted my drape, looked at me, looked again, and burst out laughing. Another tech came in, looked, looked again, and did the same.

I couldn't help it. It was too perfect. For some reason, Bob Hope popped into my head that morning, and I knew it was divine inspiration. There on my chest, I had my friend write:

"Thanks for the mammaries. . . ."

Mary Anne Breen

5

HEALING

*It's only when we truly know and understand
that we have a limited time on Earth—and
that we have no way of knowing when our
time is up—that we will begin to live each
day to the fullest, as if it was the only one
we had.*

Elisabeth Kübler-Ross

The Seasons of Our Lives

Waiting behind glass panels at the airport for a delayed flight from Honolulu, I reflect on how the world has changed since another time I had waited for my best friend. Before 9/11 and the new airport security, I could wait directly at the gate, a blessing because her e-mail that morning said test results had confirmed that the small lump found in her annual mammogram was indeed cancer.

Mary Kelly and I had met seventeen years earlier at a three-week-long motivational seminar where we'd been assigned to each other as "Perfect Partners." Our job was to keep each other on track and accountable in achieving our business goals. Her naturally ebullient nature and enthusiasm made our assignment of checking in by telephone with each other every day a joy. As our friendship and trust deepened, we realized we'd found the best friends we could each imagine.

In the years that followed, I comforted her when she went through a painful divorce and consoled her as she told me how she yearned for a storybook marriage just like mine. A few years later, she met just the right man, and as she made plans to move to Hawaii to be with him, my own husband lay dying of cancer. She buoyed my spirits then, reminding me of my many blessings and how much life I had ahead.

And now, again, it is my turn to comfort her. I can think of no way to be of real help. "Let me know if I can do anything to help you . . ." well-wishers say kindly, feeling helpless when there's not much to be done.

Rows of people exited the plane that day, and she rushed into my arms. Her husband, Don, stood to the side, looking pale and perplexed, as men often are when there is a problem they can't analyze and solve. During their visit, the four of us, including my second husband, Ted, who had lost his wife of twenty-two years to another, more virulent form of breast cancer, processed this new information together.

Ted spoke about his friend, Mo, who told him recently her breast-cancer treatment hadn't been as bad as she expected, so we called her on the phone, and she and Mary talked a long time. I heard Mary laughing, saying, "Really? You're kidding!" She later related that Mo told her she'd found chemotherapy to be a beauty treatment, saying that every cell is renewed in the process, and her skin has never looked better. How startled we were at this idea!

Mary found new resolve in our loving embrace. She told me how, because of the successful Tahitian pearl business she and Don had built together, she always finds inspiration in how the pearl oyster deals with an irritant, turning the experience into something exquisite and unique. She said she was determined to do that with the challenge ahead.

"Will you come to Hawaii and be my chemo buddy? I plan to choose someone I love to be with me for each of the sessions. Having company will give Don a break and will cheer me on." Of course I said yes.

Her sister was her first chemo buddy, and Barb cooked

what seemed like one hundred ready-to-eat meals and stored them in the freezer.

Before Christmas 2000, I arrived, prepared to sleep on a futon on the floor, with their little black cat for company. I learned Jet had his own preferences, liking to be petted as he ate. Mary was a wonder during the second treatment, stoic about any discomfort—reminiscing, confiding, loving my poring over her manuscript and making editing suggestions. I felt deeply in service, like I was making a real contribution, so her invitation to me was a gift.

Now, a year and a half later, there she is, waving as she rushes into the terminal. Skin glowing (the beauty treatment promise was true!), weight gained from the experience nearly gone, she has triumphed. And like the pearl oyster, she has produced something profoundly meaningful in dealing with breast cancer—her appreciation for life has been enriched, and she is more clearly in touch with what matters and who she is at her core.

Greeting her at the airport once more, I reflect that in the years ahead, no doubt a time will come when it will be her turn to comfort me again. Through the changing seasons of our lives, only one thing remains the same—our devotion to each other as Perfect Partners.

Diana von Welenetz Wentworth

"You're such a good friend,
you can complain first!"

Reprinted with permission of Stephanie Piro ©2004.

You've Got to Play If You Want to Win

We all have big changes in our lives that are more or less a second chance.

Harrison Ford

Since my friend Pat died in 2000, there has not been one day that I have not thought about her. To hear me say that, you'd think that she and I were really good friends ... best friends. But the truth is that Pat has played a bigger part in my life since she died than she ever did when she was alive.

We met in 1998 at a very special kind of support group. It was a dance movement therapy class, and only breast-cancer patients and survivors could sign up for it. There were just ten women admitted into the group, and we each had to commit to attend every one of the twelve classes. We were there to support and encourage each other.

Now, I had participated in other cancer support groups, but this one was different—and not only because of the commitment to the other members of the group. The name "dance movement therapy" said it all: we were not going to just sit around and talk. Fortunately, there was very little dance involved—otherwise, I wouldn't have made it through the first class! But there was a lot of movement, and that was tough enough.

That first day, I was very nervous about looking foolish in front of the other women. So, when the music started, I just stood in place—feet firmly rooted in the ground, knees locked, body stiff, eyes shut tight—swaying slightly with the beat.

When our instructor told us there were drawing materials available if we wanted to express our feelings using that medium, I was horrified. As far as I was concerned, the only thing worse than "dancing" in front of a roomful of strangers was drawing in front of a roomful of strangers. From the expressions on the other women's faces—and from the way their bodies hadn't moved either—I knew I wasn't the only one wondering how I could get out of the commitment I'd made.

But one of the women, Pat, moved with ease right from the very first moment of the very first class. She wasn't self-conscious at all about using her body to express herself in front of an audience of strangers. In fact, she seemed to be having fun. Not only that, but several times during the class, she walked over to where the art supplies were and used them. I was in awe that anyone could feel that free, that safe, showing who they really were and how they felt in front of a group of strangers. My desire to feel that comfortable kept me coming back every week. That, and the promise I'd made when joining the group.

By the end of the twelve weeks, with Pat as our role model, we danced, moved, wrote group poetry, drew and played with each other without a second thought. It wasn't a surprise, considering our comfort level, when, several months later, Pat called all of us to say that she had been diagnosed with metastases to her bones and liver.

She asked if we would form a special kind of support group for her, for as long as she needed it.

Most of us said yes, and Pat's healing circle (which is how we referred to ourselves) met each month at different homes, with the original members from the dance movement therapy class. By the time Pat died almost two years later, there was a loyal group of five who were there for her every month.

In the beginning, because this was new for us—and, after all, what had happened to Pat could happen to any of us—we were very serious. Our monthly get-togethers would start with a potluck dinner, and then we would solemnly do light massage and other hands-on work on Pat while chanting or calling her name. It was a somber and dark experience.

Before long, just as in dance movement therapy class, with Pat leading the way, we loosened up. She said she was open to whatever the group wanted to do, so we started having theme nights. Once we each brought a video and voted on which one to watch. We drummed or toned or sculpted with clay or made masks. One time we went on a field trip to walk a labyrinth. When Pat lost her hair again, we decorated bald caps—and each of us wore one. The same night, we hennaed her bald head. And, of course, we played music and moved and danced. No matter what we did, Pat was game. She was always the most enthusiastic of us all.

During the time we got together, sometimes Pat felt great, and sometimes she felt terrible. But, no matter how she felt, she was there, physically and in every other way. Her light-heartedness, her open attitude to embrace all that life had to offer and her willingness to play gave the rest of us permission to be the same way. And so, instead of being somber, serious and self-conscious, Pat's healing circle became a respite of light and joy and fun. We played.

During the last two weeks of Pat's life, there wasn't a day when one of us was not with her. And, at her memorial service, fittingly called a celebration of life, the healing circle was there. I spoke and sang in church, in front of complete strangers and, along with the rest of the members of Pat's healing circle, I danced my heart out. In front of all those people we had never seen before in our lives, we played in Pat's honor.

I don't know where Pat was born or where she grew up. I don't know what her favorite color was or what her favorite song was. I don't know if she was a Democrat or a Republican, and I have no idea if she went to church. Our friendship wasn't like that.

Pat and I—we were heart friends. We had a connection that came from the soul, a place where no one is self-conscious, no one is afraid to look foolish. It is a place where you can use words or music or art or movement or touch to show how you feel.

A few months after Pat's death, I joined another dance movement therapy class with nine other women, all of whom were strangers. Right from the very first moment of the very first class, when the music came on I was moving around the room with ease. I wasn't self-conscious at all about using my body to express myself in front of an audience of strangers. In fact, I was having fun. I couldn't believe how free, how safe, I felt showing who I really was and how I really felt. When the music stopped, I used the art supplies, and I knew then that Pat had helped me much more than I had ever helped her.

Every day since she died, I hear Pat's voice saying to me, "Remember to play." And I play. I play.

Lori Misicka

A "Gift of Healing" Journey

*No journey carries one far unless, as it extends
into the world around us, it goes an equal dis-
tance into the world within.*

                                                    Lillian Smith

Little did I know that following my breast-cancer diagnosis in June 1989 that I would go on a fantastic, life-
enhancing, healing journey. It's hard to believe that cancer
can be a gift in a person's life. It is in mine, although it did-
n't happen right away. I had all the shock and fears, and I
was so afraid that I couldn't even pray for myself, but I
reached out to everyone whom I thought could help me.

My first call was to Reach to Recovery with the
American Cancer Society. Next, I called Mitz Aoki, a professor at the University of Hawaii, who ministered to
those with life-threatening illnesses. Through prayer and
guided imagery, he turned my focus away from fear and
into looking into our Lord's face to see peace within me—
and see myself healing.

I created a team of loving people and a healing environ-
ment around me—medically, spiritually, emotionally and

physically. In his book, *Love, Medicine and Miracles*, Bernie Siegel calls people like me "exceptional cancer patients." He says we can't only rely on doctors to help us; we play a major part in our healing. I began to feel I could be in control of my life again—a feeling I had lost.

I also started to journal. I wrote down all the scary stuff, the frustrations, the mountain-top and valley experiences. It meant so much to me to reread it later—to see where I had been and how far I had come.

I found a cancer support group at a local church led by a woman who was recovering from breast cancer. She, too, used guided imagery that she had composed and shared. She took us, in our imaginations, to places where we could feel comfortable, peaceful and safe—on a beach chair by the ocean, a flowering garden, beside a gentle, trickling stream. We were relaxed, refreshed and restored.

The cancer support group became a part of my life, and our leader asked me to take over the group when her breast cancer recurred. Creating my own meditations and prayers, and ministering to my brothers and sisters, was where I wanted and needed to be. At that point I realized my healing journey had become a "gift" to me. I had my eyes open for other ways to share my "gift" on my healing journey.

In 1996, I took a class on energy centers of the body that was offered for interested volunteers at Queen's Medical Center. It is called Healing Touch as it is a hands-on type of complementary medicine, and I asked to volunteer in the radiation therapy department so I could be there for cancer patients. I see the patients in the waiting room, their faces full of concern, and I invite them to have Healing Touch in a room where we have a bed set aside. I play soft music and pray silently or aloud, whichever the person prefers. I show how to relax body and mind, and by placing my hand over the energy centers, bring mind, body and spirit back into peace, harmony and wellness.

I began to introduce guided imagery into our sessions when several patients wished they could have a private cassette tape of our sessions. I asked them in their imaginations to go to a special place of their own, using all their senses, and describe the scene to me. I would write down all their words. The tape began with relaxation, and then I would repeat back to them the thoughts and the scene they had chosen, along with reinforcing, healing words. Their faces were peaceful, sometimes with a gentle smile. One patient went to her favorite childhood park to swing higher and higher; another went to a vacation on the beach in Bali with warm tradewinds; another went hang-gliding over Makapuu Beach, soaring for two hours. They were really there, no doubt in my mind. Energetic, but peaceful, they experienced a sense of well-being that the body acknowledged and responded with healing.

I became a participant in the bosom buddies program under Healing Touch about four years ago. We adopt a breast-cancer patient and serve her for six months in any way we can. I have had four bosom buddies, and my first was an exceptional cancer patient. She always had a notebook with her at our sessions. She said she was an author and wanted to write a book. I'm sure she has.

My latest quest has been to create and record a CD of relaxation and guided imagery for all patients in our department and any other hospital patient who wants one. Our patients are well on their way into their healing journey as we provide them with healing tools to help themselves—a respite in times of need.

We are here on Earth to love and take care of each other, and I'm deeply honored to share my "gift of healing" wherever I can. I am truly blessed.

Betsy Ludwig

Isabelle and Her Dollies' Hair

Each day comes bearing its own gifts. Untie the ribbons.

Ruth Ann Schabacker

When the oncologist outlined my treatment following two breast-cancer surgeries, I was most fearful of the chemotherapy and the promise I would lose my hair. I'd bought two fashionable wigs (which I never wore) and asked my hair stylist if she would cut my hair very short. In spite of all my preparations, I was in complete denial of the inevitable and hoped somehow it wouldn't happen to me.

I was told I would have sixteen weeks of chemotherapy (eight weeks of Cytoxan and Adriamycin and eight weeks of Taxol), to be followed by six weeks of daily radiation. Sixteen days after my first chemotherapy, my hair began to come out in huge clumps. True reality set in; not only was I feeling physically unwell, but with hair loss I plunged into emotional despair.

My husband sweetly offered to clip the few remaining strands that clung to my scalp, but a friend frankly told me to deal with reality and have all that remained cut off, which my husband did. I was now totally bald—and it was just as tough an assignment for him as for me.

I was determined to get this stage of my treatment over with as quickly as sixteen weeks could go, and I resolved to stay as healthy as possible. I followed all the directives and avoided crowds, ate as well as I could—even though my appetite was practically nonexistent—but the worst part was not seeing my grandchildren because I feared I might catch a cold or the flu.

My friends knew this was a very difficult time because I truly love all four grandchildren and so enjoy their company, but staying healthy and infection-free was a great incentive because I longed for their sweet faces and amazing wisdom.

Chemo treatments ended on schedule, without interruption, and I looked forward to my first celebration with family, friends and four grandchildren at Thanksgiving. Even though I wasn't feeling well and was still very bald, I wore a hat and cautiously prepared to see my family, some of whom had not seen the "new" me, who had lost twenty-five pounds (not counting the missing hair). I was anxious about how my grandchildren, ages three to six, would feel . . . and I didn't want to scare them.

Thanksgiving was perfect in every way. How grateful I was to be back with my marvelous family and part of a social circle again! The children were all far less concerned by my appearance than I was; they were curious and innocently intrigued by my bald head. Grace, age four, simply proclaimed that I should have put my "old hair" under my pillow, and with true Tooth Fairy magic, my new hair would reappear the next day. The children cautiously touched my head, and I just assumed their simple behavior was a very accepting way to deal with my unusual appearance.

When one of my walking friends asked me the next

week how everything had gone, I was happy to report, "The day was uneventful, and I felt completely at ease, not really aware that any of the children were affected by my appearance."

It wasn't until six weeks later, when I had a head of soft down, that my daughter Sara presented me with a photograph and told me what Isabelle, my three-year-old granddaughter, had done. Isabelle had secretively kept to herself in her room and was unusually quiet for a surprising amount of time. Sara, an exceptionally patient mother, entered her daughter's room to discover the child cutting off her doll's hair! Surprised by Isabelle's actions, Sara discovered that over a period of three days, Isabelle had trimmed the hair of each of her three dolls, including Ariel, the red-headed Disney mermaid. Calmly, she asked Isabelle what she was doing.

Very matter-of-factly, Isabelle said, "I needed to have them be just like Mew-Mew," the name she calls me.

Paula Young

The Bus Ride

An individual doesn't get cancer, a family does.

Terry Tempest Williams

Five afternoons each week, the rickety old shuttle bus opens its doors to a waiting group of radiation patients. The door creaks shut and, with windows and bones rattling, the bus and its cargo bump along four freeways to the Kaiser Permanente Cancer Center in Los Angeles.

Stories, shared experiences and traumas unite these strangers thrown suddenly together. My wife, Catherine, is one of them.

Rider: "Is that a Walkman?"

Catherine: "Yes, it is. My husband bought it for me when I started riding this bus."

Rider: "Sounds like you got yourself quite a man."

Catherine: "Yes, he is. I appreciate him so very much."

Rider: "Wow, I've gotta get me one of those."

Catherine: "Don't give up that thought—he may be just around the corner."

Rider: "What are you talking about?"

Catherine: "The possibility of a husband."

Rider: "Husband! I don't want no husband, honey. I've already tried on one of those. I was talking about getting a Walkman. Now that's what I call useful."

Catherine and I are in this thing together, and we have been ever since the doctor looked at the first suspect mammogram, sending us on a journey that has drawn us closer than ever before, even if I'm not on that daily ride. There's nothing like a traumatic personal event to test the fabric of a relationship; out of that test, I suspect, comes one change or another—perhaps for better or worse. I can't imagine everything remaining the same.

Her first lumpectomy involved the placement of a marker wire clear through the right breast, and then removal of tissue, including a lump that sat against the chest wall. Before the surgery, the surgeon had said, "The signs are all in your favor. Let's get this over with."

I answered the phone when he called a couple of days later with the pathology report. "It's cancer," he said. There was more, but those first words floored me, and I felt tears well in my eyes.

Catherine said, "Tell me everything. Don't leave anything out."

"He said a second surgery is needed to remove more tissue and several lymph nodes." She listened and said simply, "Oh, I see."

We believe in stepping into the fire of life with both eyes open, and we looked at each other for awhile without needing to speak.

Her second surgery was scheduled to last one hour. An hour and ten minutes later, the surgeon hadn't shown up, and I was very concerned.

Finally, he appeared. "Hi, John. You doing okay? Yes, the operation is now complete. No, it didn't take too long . . . sometimes it's longer, sometimes shorter, and she's safely in the recovery room now. There were no complications or problems—the surgery was a thing well done." Whew. Relief flooded every cell. Up, down, up, down, up. As long as we land on "up," I'll be fine.

A cancer patient's life is filled with the unexpected. Every day is a walk along a new learning path for the whole family. Patients often get used to it, even gaining a morbid sense of humor, as evidenced by this exchange Catherine heard on her daily bus adventure:

Rider 1: "I don't want to get on this bus one more day. It's driving me out of my mind, and I don't want to do this anymore."

Rider 2 (hands on hips, eyes twinkling): "Dearie, you get on that bus this instant! Get on that bus or die!"

Rider 1 (smiling sweetly, as she gets on the bus): "Thank you. I needed that."

No one chooses to have cancer. It leaves a cloud hovering over one's life because the outcome is never certain. But then . . . what is?

It is also a gift.

When Catherine was bed-ridden after each of the surgeries, I lovingly took care of her. Spending more time at home, I had the opportunity to look around and appreciate the pleasures and treasures that are mine: our faithful dog, the richly stocked library, the lovely kitchen, the bed of recovery, the couch of conviviality, the garden of dynamic life, and—most important—my healing wife. Being here is what I choose.

For us, John and Catherine, this is the time of living intensely. Out go the previous habits of a lifetime that don't serve, either because they never did or because they no longer do.

In come those things that allow us to grow, to delve deeply into this life . . . and lead to happiness. We became better listeners, clearer speakers, more thoughtful discerners and quicker to smile in recognition of life's joys. Somewhere, somehow, I was given this life that is so beautifully enmeshed with the life of another. It's a blessing.

John de Strakosch

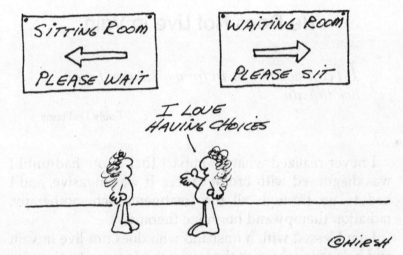

He Does Not Live in Vain

If I can stop one heart from breaking, I shall not live in vain.

Emily Dickinson

I never realized what an impact that quote had until I was diagnosed with breast cancer. It was invasive, and I had to go through all the treatments—chemotherapy, radiation therapy and hormone therapy.

I am blessed with a husband who does not live in vain and helped me through the treatment. I was forty-six years old, and Stan and I had only been married two months.

There was one definite: I would lose all my silky, strawberry-blonde hair—my crowning glory—the source of many compliments and much joy for me. The thought of being bald, even for a short period of time, saddened me.

Three weeks after the first injection, my hair was coming out by the handfuls. I was sitting in front of our bathroom mirror crying as hard as I ever had. Stan heard me and came to find out what was the matter.

He put his hands on my shoulders and asked me, "What's wrong, honey?"

"I don't want you to wake up every morning and see me bald."

My husband, who is bald, smiled and said, "But you wake up every morning and see me that way."

Of all the words in the world, none have ever meant more to me. I still cried, but now more with the joy of having the love of this man than of losing my hair. I will never doubt how much he loves me.

I'm happy to say that I'm now a nine-year survivor, a result of modern technological advances, wonderful medical personnel, a strong constitution, great faith and a man who "does not live in vain."

Suzanne Metzger

Stop Changing!

The Real Voyage of Discovery comes not in see-
ing new landscapes, but in having new eyes.

Marcel Proust

As I pulled away from Mark Twain Elementary School, I observed the laughing school kids tumbling into waiting cars, daycare vans and school buses. Their tightly held homework sheets flapped in the almost autumn wind.

I glanced into the rearview mirror and smiled. *I love this time of day,* I thought to myself.

Ashley and Garrett, my two step-children, sat in the back seat under a pile of backpacks and lunchboxes. They smelled of orange peels, peanut butter and playground dust.

I'm so glad to be part of this family, I thought.

Ashley's ponytail was loose, her red hair falling string-straight across her freckled face. In the mirror, I caught her eye. "Hey, do you like my new hair color?"

She shrugged and then nodded. Garrett turned away from me and looked a little harder out the window. I didn't really expect them to approve. After all, when I dropped them off for school this morning, I was dishwater blonde. Then, without warning, I bought a box of midnight ebony at the grocery store. Two or three hours later and voila! My hair was now the deep black I'd always envied on my edgy, artistic friends.

A crossing guard stopped traffic in front of us, near the intersection of Greencove and Glenville Drive. A group of the neighborhood girls skipped by in light-up tennis shoes and vibrant jackets. Waiting for the parade to reach the far curb, I let my eyes linger on the rearview mirror. Still no smile from the silence behind me. *Not surprising,* I reasoned. Ashley and Garrett had lived through a divorce, adjusted to new step-parents and made a difficult transition from their mother's house to ours. Then, just when life must have felt predictable again, I was diagnosed with breast cancer.

"Hey, if you don't like this new hue," I continued, emphasizing the rhyme to lighten things up, "the good thing is, my hair is going to fall out soon anyway." I giggled, turning to Garrett, playfully, "And then . . . I'm going to get a tattoo on my bald head!"

He snapped back to the world inside our car, fiercely locking his eyes onto mine. "Stop changing!" he demanded. "Don't lose your hair! Don't get a tattoo! I'll be in third grade before it grows back."

As stunned as we were by his outburst, Ashley spoke first. "Garrett," she said softly, comforting him in the motherly tone she had perfected, "it's okay. It's okay."

My mind was racing. *Why is he so upset?* My hair was waist-length when I first met the kids. For our wedding, it was bobbed at the shoulder. Then last month, it got shorter, much shorter. Change. Change. Change. Now, it was a different color. More change.

Then it hit me. Garrett's desperation revealed my own hidden fear. *For the first time in my life, I am faced with something I cannot control . . . and I am terrified.* Breast cancer changed things without my permission, changed things that I didn't want to change. Cutting, coloring, tattooing— these things helped sustain the illusion that I decided what would happen to my body, that I was in control.

In the driveway, the kids squeezed out of the car. I shouldered my briefcase, picked up Ashley's pink backpack and reached for Garrett's hand.

"After supper, would you guys help me and your dad pick out a wig?"

"*Not* red," Ashley said.

"Like your hair was before?" Garrett asked.

"Yeah, maybe," I said. "The catalog has lots of choices. Maybe one will be like mine was before."

We walked into the house together. It was a good feeling, knowing what would probably happen next, able to predict that after supper we would all sit down together and choose a wig, then brush our teeth, read a book and go to sleep.

I love this time of day, I thought. I'm so glad to be part of this family.

Rhonda Richards-Cohen

"Shoot the Messengers"

No matter how difficult, it might be a pearl in the making.

Don Kelly

When bad news comes like a thunderclap, it's hard to imagine good can come of it.

Two years ago, I went with my wife to hear the results of her biopsy. A routine mammogram had indicated something suspicious, the ultrasound confirmed it, and she had a needle biopsy. I accompanied her to hear the results, even though we both knew there could be nothing wrong with her—she was so healthy! She squeezed my hand tight as we entered the radiation offices, bent on keeping our positive attitude.

We sat in the hallway for five to ten minutes, and then were called in to a storage room filled with unused X-ray equipment. We sat on cold steel stools against a cement wall on a cement floor in an icy-cold air-conditioned room.

The technician wasted no time. She looked my wife straight in the eye and said, "It is cancer."

We both sat there in shock. I asked, "Couldn't there be some mistake?"

"No mistake," she said coldly. "It's cancer. It's definitely cancer."

We were paralyzed, our mouths dry, unable to speak for several minutes. Tears made a path down my wife's cheeks. Finally, we stood up and walked like zombies down the cold hallway and out of the office. On the way to the car, I said, "Cruel! She was cold and cruel and almost seemed to enjoy telling us in a sadistic way." Although it can never be an easy task to tell someone she or he has cancer, we both agreed there had to be a better way.

The surgeon's office had closed early that day, so we hadn't talked to her doctor. We didn't know the gravity of the diagnosis; we had no details about the size, grade or seriousness of the cancer.

We went home to bed, and I held her as we both cried. We lay there a long time, holding hands, trying to assimilate the terrifying news. We talked about finances, our will; my wife was picking out her gravestone. Actually, she decided on cremation.

All this torture was unnecessary. Nobody told us that most people survive breast cancer. The technician who delivered the dire message suggested nothing positive, no books, no reading material, no support groups. Nothing. We were left to our own resources, stumbling in the dark to find out what choices we had.

As we lay there that night, we thought, *With all the money that goes into research and equipment, wouldn't it have been nice if we had been taken into a comfortable seating area, been greeted by a professional counselor whose job is to convey the news to people, as well as their many options and choices?*

After that first night, having successfully weathered the "knock-out punch," we called our friend and teacher on

Kauai, Dr. Serge King, who specializes in Aloha Spirit and healing, using ancient Hawaiian practices. He informed us that he had developed a new technique called the Dynamind treatment. We flew to see him and had a session right away. He sat across from my wife and asked her if she was having any emotional feelings about her cancer. She couldn't come up with anything, but then suddenly said, "I feel like I'm ruining our wonderful life."

"There's no reason for those feelings of guilt," he said. "Let's get rid of them. The Dynamind treatment can make an incredible difference by releasing stored emotions in the space of a minute. You first acknowledge the problem, relax the mind, fill the body with breath and energy, and use physical touch and kinesiology to redirect the mind."

He continued, "Repeat after me: I'm feeling some guilt about my cancer and that can change. I want that feeling of guilt to change. I want that to go away now."

She repeated what he said.

"Now tap your fingers seven times on the breastbone at the center of the chest, then seven times on the area between your left thumb and index finger, now seven times on the right hand, then seven times on the base of the neck. Now take a deep breath and tell me on a scale of ten, ten being the worst and one being the least, how are you feeling about the guilt?"

My wife took a deep breath, opened her eyes and said, "It's about a seven."

"Okay," he said, "let's do it again. Take a deep breath and do it again."

She went through the series again, took a deep breath and said, "It's about a four."

"Well, then, let's do it once more," Serge said.

She went through the process one more time, and at the end she took a deep breath and said, "It's gone."

"Do you feel anything else? Sadness or anger at the cancer?"

"A little fear."

"Whenever that comes up, take a deep breath and say, 'I'm feeling a little anxiety, and that can change. I want that anxiety to change. I want it to go away now.'"

We were overjoyed to have something positive and constructive to use in our healing.

As my wife went through numerous scary tests and treatments, this technique was immensely helpful and gave her the willpower to overcome her challenges.

When she was feeling nauseous after surgery, she was able to use the technique to overcome it. She went on to use the technique over and over again, through eight rounds of chemotherapy, seven weeks of radiation, hair loss, weight gain from steroids and other difficult side effects.

She has emerged on the other side of the tunnel, more beautiful than ever. She found some great books like *Chicken Soup for the Survivor's Soul; Living Beyond Breast Cancer, A Survivor's Guide; Uplift: Secrets from the Sisterhood of Breast Cancer Survivors; Hope Is Contagious; Not Just One in Eight;* and many others. She even wrote a book called *Path of the Pearl: Discover Your Treasures Within,* about the way a pearl oyster takes an irritant and transforms it into something of great rarity and beauty—a pearl. I came up with a phrase that sums up her book and her medical journey: "No matter how difficult, it might be a pearl in the making."

Glowing with health, her energy returned, we both give thanks for the gifts of this journey. We appreciate every day of our lives that we have together. We take nothing for granted. We feel blessed—we've been given a second chance. We both feel a deep commitment to helping others get through their breast-cancer journey. We believe in utilizing all the support that is available—great Web sites, helpful books, local support groups, alternative healing along with Western medicine, and plenty of positive tools and techniques.

There is a lot of help out there! Make use of *all* the excellent support that's available and then perhaps you won't have to "shoot the messenger."

Don Kelly

"He's looking for his wife, but she's been taking
all those life-saving breast cancer treatments and he's
not sure when she might be able to get away."

Angel Hugh

If you are going through hell, keep going.

Sir Winston Churchill

"Try my feet," I groaned. "I've got some good veins there." The IV needle in my hand had stopped working, and an exhausted young doctor was unsuccessfully trying to insert a new one. She had been at it for half an hour. At midnight on a Friday, she was the only doctor on duty in the oncology ward of this National Health Service hospital in central London, and for me, she was the only game in town. I knew she'd been on duty for far too many hours, but I didn't really care. I had my own problems.

"I'll give you one more shot at it, then I'm done. I'll drink the damn blood, the antibiotics, the acyclovir, whatever you want. But after this one, I've had enough." I gritted my teeth, grabbed the cold iron bed frame and tried not to cry out. Vampira dug around, looking for a vein on my foot. She stabbed. She stabbed again.

"I can't do this," and she stood, hands shaking. "I've done twenty of these today, and I did them perfectly well. You've had so much chemo, your veins just won't cooperate." She angrily pulled the curtain back and stomped out into the ward.

I had an infection in the central line they had surgically implanted in my chest, as well as an adverse reaction to my first high dose of chemotherapy. My white blood count had dropped, and a fever had gone so high that it gave me the shakes. I was at the nadir of my nadir. And all I wanted now was for it all to stop. All of it.

The last weeks had seen me in and out of the hospital in preparation for the high doses of chemotherapy I was soon to receive. Each visit meant a different bed, a different view of the same gray-green walls and mostly different faces. Unlike American hospitals with their double or triple patient rooms, this was one large ward, with approximately twenty beds separated only by the curtains you were allowed to draw around. It was a mixed sex ward, but we had all lost our modesty along with our privacy. Personal dignity had somehow ceased to matter.

Most of my fellow patients were asleep, and I sat in my curtained cubicle, legs crossed, a red velvet hat on my bald head, listening to their snores and grunts. I dreaded the next chapter of my nightmare and had stopped trying to imagine just where the plot was headed.

Suddenly, the ward sister flung my curtain wide. "This is Hugh from the intensive care unit." And she was gone.

"Nice hat," Hugh said with a grin, as he gently pulled the curtain shut.

"Bet you're bald as a coot under there." I tried to smile.

"May I?" and he took a seat beside me on the bed. "What's the problem?" He looked me over, as though buying a used car. "I see a lot of places we can get a needle in." He counted the little Band-aids plastered over all the failed attempts on my arm and hand. "Thirteen," he exclaimed in wonder.

I shook my head. "You missed my feet."

He shook his head back at me. "And before every one, the doc said, 'This won't hurt a bit.' Right?" He laughed. "You ever hear the one about the guy who wanted to castrate his cat?"

I shook my head, slower this time. Was this guy going to tell me a joke?

Didn't he have a life to save, a phone call to make, a nap to take?

Hugh continued. "He didn't have any money to go to the vet, so his best friend tells him, 'I'll do it for you. It's simple. You hold the cat. I get a couple of bricks, and I hold 'em one in each hand. Like this. When the cat's nice and calm, I do this.' And the best friend slams the two bricks together. The cat owner is appalled. 'Won't that hurt?' he whispered. 'Oh, no,' replied the best friend. 'Not as long as I remember to keep my thumbs up.'"

Hugh grinned even wider. And I laughed for the first time in days, as much at his enjoyment as at the joke.

In a low, conspiratorial voice, he went on, "So the doc was right. It didn't hurt her a bit." I laughed again. "Now I'm going to numb this bit of your hand with a little cream, and we'll wait a minute for it to work. No need for any more pain than you have already, right?" We waited.

Hugh cocked his head. "They tell me you're having a hard time?" A pause, and he continued. "I had a Jeep accident in Africa a few years ago. My girlfriend and my friend were killed, and I was in the hospital for six months. It was a pretty dark time. It might have been something like what you're going through now." He was almost whispering.

"You don't want to do this anymore, do you?" I nodded, hesitantly. It was hard to admit in a world that admired fighters that I wanted to quit, to give up, to give in.

"I always compare it to *mal de mer*. You know, seasickness? When you're in the middle of a channel crossing to

France, and the boat is heaving, and you're being sick over the side, all you want is for it to stop. You just want to die. But when you get to the other side, you can't believe you ever felt that way."

Hugh looked straight into my eyes. "You're going to get to the other side of this, and you won't believe you ever felt the way you've felt tonight."

I could feel my tears. "Now, let's get this needle in. There. Done. Perfect." And it was.

He stood to go. "If you have any more trouble, have them page me, and if I'm in the hospital, I'll come." He stopped at the curtain and turned back. "I'm not a very good fortune teller, but I'm a heck of a good bookie. You know what I say? You're going to make it." With that, he was gone.

It's now seven years since I finished my high-dose chemotherapy and the radiotherapy that followed. My health remains robust, and though others may say I am in "remission," I consider myself "cured." Out of my experience came my first play, "Gone to L.A.," a black comedy about breast cancer, which will be made into a film later this year. In it, one of my favorite characters refers to "Angel Hugh from ICU," the guy who can "cannulate your friggin' earlobe."

When "Gone to L.A." opened at the Hampstead Theatre in London, I was pleased that a great number of the family and friends who helped me through my illness were among the audience. It made me laugh inside to know that Angel Hugh was one of them.

Lolly Susi

6

COURAGE

The only courage that matters is the kind that gets you from one moment to the next.

Mignon McLaughlin

Knowing What Your Rope Is

When you get to the end of your rope—tie a knot in it and hang on.

Eleanor Roosevelt

Shortly after learning I had a rare kind of breast cancer that would require a year of aggressive treatments, I decided to cut back on some of my activities.

I stopped by my son's classroom to explain to his teacher why I would no longer be coming to help every Monday morning. When I became upset as I told her about my diagnosis and the long months of treatment that lay ahead, she took my hands, held them tightly and told me this story about her friend, Ann.

One summer, Ann decided to go river rafting. Everyone who signed up for the trip had to learn the basic procedures and safety measures. As the instructor outlined the dangers, Ann became scared. What if her raft capsized or was dashed against the rocks? What if she were thrown into the rapidly churning water and carried downstream before anyone could rescue her?

The instructor had one answer to all of Ann's anxious

questions: "There is a rope that is attached to the perime-
ter of the raft. Whatever happens, hold on to that rope.
Never let go. Just hold on." And do you know what? An
unexpected storm came up, and Ann's raft did capsize,
but she remembered her instructor's words. She held on
to that rope, and she survived.

I stared at my friend, wondering what this had to do
with me. "Know what your rope is, Myra," she counseled.
"And hold on—to whatever it is. Through whatever happens, just keep holding on."

She gave me a hug and returned to her classroom, leaving me to ponder her words. What was my rope? What
would I hold on to in the days ahead? What would help
me survive my perilous journey through surgery? It did-
n't take me long to find the answer. My rope would be the
love of my family and friends, which I knew would support me through whatever lay ahead.

As my treatment progressed, that rope was often at
hand. It was there during my chemotherapy when my
husband said, "Lean on me. I'll be here to give you
strength. If you can't go on, I'll carry you until you're
strong enough to continue on your own."

It was there the day of my surgery when a dear friend
hung a silk carp, the Japanese symbol of courage, in my
hospital room. It was there on Mother's Day when, unsure
of what lay ahead, my daughter gave me an opal, the symbol of hope. And it was there one night after I had lost my
hair, when I found fifty cents under my pillow with a note
from the "hair fairy."

There were times during the year when I didn't get
along with the people whose closeness and support I so
desperately needed. I argued with my children about their
refusal to attend a support group for families dealing with
cancer. I fought with my husband over the handling of
certain household matters.

In the past, I had been able to handle disagreements such as these easily, but at this particular time, I couldn't tolerate the feelings of loneliness and isolation that followed arguments. On these occasions, it felt as though the rope was slipping out of my hands, and I feared the dark waters would engulf me. These were the most frightening days of all because I knew I couldn't make it through a year of treatment alone. The love and laughter of my family and friends were just as essential to my survival as the chemotherapy and radiation treatments.

I discovered that Aristotle was right when he said, "Friendship is a thing most necessary to life, since without friends, no one would choose to live, though possessed of all other advantages."

And so throughout the entire year, I held on. I held on when it appeared as though my tumor wasn't shrinking as it was supposed to in response to the chemotherapy. I held on when a bone scan revealed a dark spot that looked suspiciously like bone cancer on a rib. I held on as though my life depended on it, because it did.

I survived my journey. My raft, although battered by storms and raging currents, is still afloat. I often hear my friend's words echoing in my mind: "Know what your rope is, Myra." I do, and I'm still holding on.

Myra Shostak

A Message from My Marine

My chemotherapy and radiation treatments were finally over, and I had begun the long, slow process of physical, emotional and spiritual healing. I continued to have a great deal of pain from one of the chemotherapy drugs, and my oncologist told me it could be many months before the pain subsided. The throbbing in my bones was a constant, annoying reminder that I was not yet fully recovered.

During this time, my older son joined the United States Marine Corps. Initially I was disappointed that he had chosen not to go to college right away, and, of course, I was worried for his safety, but I was also immensely proud of his decision and his courage. The day I saw him graduate from recruit training at Parris Island, South Carolina, is one of the proudest days of my life.

During his training at Parris Island (one of the most grueling of boot camps in the armed forces), he sent me a letter describing some of what he was experiencing. He told of the biting sand fleas that infested the island. He told of ten-mile training runs in sweltering heat and humidity and the resulting blisters on his feet that broke and bled. He told of taking a pounding from another recruit in a boxing exercise.

The most amazing thing about the letter, however, was that not one word of my son's detailed account held even a hint of complaint! He was clearly (and deservedly) proud of himself and his fellow recruits, and marveling each and every day at how much discomfort and even excruciating pain they could withstand. He was on a journey of self-discovery, testing his physical and mental limits, and reaching beyond them.

The letter ended with these words: "Mom, remember that pain is just weakness leaving your body."

What powerful words those were! I clung to them and made them my mantra. I wrote them on an index card and taped it where I could see it every day.

With the words of my son's letter and the attitude they mirrored, the way in which I looked at my pain shifted. It no longer meant that I was ill. It meant that I was alive, and that weakness and disease were leaving my body.

From the day I received that letter to this very minute, I have found discomfort and pain of every kind to be easier to bear if I just remind myself of my son's brave words and courageous spirit.

Kathy Cawthon

My Red Badges of Courage

Only when you truly inhabit your body can you begin the healing journey.

Gabrielle Roth

That morning, I struggled with what I was wearing, knowing I'd be out on the basketball court with other young moms, all those healthy people who might look sideways at my angry red scars and be offended. I thought about changing clothes, but I really didn't want to and didn't have the time, so I decided to go as I was and face the stares. I'd faced stares before.

After the game, my kids and I went to a department store to buy my eight-year-old some basketball shoes.

I was wearing a tank top under a zippered sweatshirt, and hadn't realized that my purse, which out of habit I'd slung over my right shoulder, pulled my sweatshirt open. My scars were easily visible to anyone who might be paying attention. The saleslady was paying attention.

We were hunched over, looking for the right shoe size among the boxes stacked under the display, when she stood up and looked at me with a serious expression.

She said, "Can I ask you a personal question?"

"Yes," I said, though not really knowing why.

She asked, very quietly, "Is that a surgery scar?"

"Yes, it is." I knew exactly what she meant as she started to ask, "Did you have surgery for . . . can . . . ?"

She didn't finish her question, so I did: "Cancer? Yes, I had breast cancer." I glanced over her shoulder briefly, just in time to see a woman look at me and then duck down, pretending to look at a pair of shoes she'd spotted.

"And . . . did you . . . beat it?" she asked, almost whispering.

"Yes, I did," I smiled back at her.

Then she reached up and lightly touched a finger to her own breast and softly said, "Last month I found a lump. I don't know what to do about it."

I paused, slight tears welling into my eyes. "You need to have this checked immediately." I reached out and touched her arm gently.

"I'm scared to find out if it is cancer."

My thoughts darted to that day a lifetime ago when I found my lump while in the shower and convinced myself it was just a cyst. I didn't want to know either. I have since learned that fear is never a reason for not doing something, and I told her as much, adding that she would very likely find out that the lump is benign. I asked, "Wouldn't you rather have it checked and know that it's nothing so you could relax?"

"Are a cyst and cancer different?"

"Yes, they are very different. And if you get it checked this week and find out that it is cancer, well then, you very likely have found it in time to beat it."

"Oh . . ." was all she could manage to say.

"Unfortunately, I waited six months after finding my lump before going to get it checked out. I sometimes wonder, if I had gone earlier, if I would have avoided a complete mastectomy or chemotherapy or radiation." She only nodded, wide eyes glancing down to my chest.

"Where should I start?"

"Go to your gynecologist, who will first do a manual exam and, if the lump seems suspicious, will send you to a lab for a mammogram. You'll be well taken care of from there one way or another. Please ... promise me that you'll go this week."

She nodded, then seemed embarrassed and turned to move away, muttering that she needed to see to other customers.

Smiling, I said, "That's fine," and added, "and I need to thank you for something. If I have helped you because you saw my scar, then it was worth letting you and anyone else notice it." She let out a soft cry and briefly put her head down before looking back up to smile at me.

That evening as my husband and I talked while making dinner, I shared this story. He declared, "Darn right you should show those scars. They are medals of honor. You fought and won a heck of a war." Yes, I did, and from that day to this, I proudly show my scars, my Red Badges of Courage.

Donna St. Jean Conti

Courage Comes in All Colors

There is more here than meets the eye.

Lady Murasaki

Two weeks after I was diagnosed with breast cancer, there was a silent auction at our church. I'd been on the committee that was putting the party together, and I knew what a great event it was going to be: great music, great food, and a room full of people feeling festive and spending money for a good cause. Our theme was "Black and White, Starry Night" and, like the famed Black and White Ball, everyone would wear either black or white. For months, while working on the invitations and soliciting donations, I'd envisioned myself wearing my favorite black-tie outfit. My husband loved it, and I always felt grown-up when I wore it—wise and worldly and sexy— and it was black as night.

But I was scheduled to have a lumpectomy five days after the event—a procedure where a breast surgeon takes a slice of tissue from your breast, as if from an orange or an apple pie—and somehow a black dress didn't feel right. I realized this would be the last public and formal event I'd ever attend with both breasts still intact.

I have, over the years, grown rather attached to my breasts. When I was in high school and college, I didn't think much about them—they were average B-cup breasts, so what was there to think? They didn't bounce too much when I played tennis, they filled out any dress or shirt I chose to wear, became marginally tender once a month, and were two of the primary reasons my boyfriend was able to say he liked my curves. The process of pregnancy, breastfeeding and motherhood, however, gave my breasts a whole new level of value. It made them, for one thing, a cup size bigger. They were plump and full, which made that same boyfriend—now my husband—pay even more attention, which was flattering and fun. Making babies also made my breasts functional. I breastfed both children for nine months each and was proud I could produce all those antibodies, all that concentrated protein.

I was three years past breastfeeding when cancer was diagnosed, and down a breast size from finally losing the weight of childbearing, so my breasts were, in some ways, past their prime. I didn't need them to please a man because Rob now knew there was far more to me than just my curves. For all practical intents and purposes, I didn't need my breasts to go on living a happy and healthy life, but the lumpectomy was still going to do them damage— and damage to your own flesh isn't something you can just offhandedly accept.

The night of the party started out at a frantic pace—I was left with just ten minutes to get dressed. I ran into the house, went to pull out the dress and stopped. Hanging next to the black velvet was a long, luxurious raspberry-red gown with a deep V-neck in front and a deeper V in back. I'd never worn it.

I bought the dress with my sister, for no good reason, on

sale at a little boutique. I had put on the Nicole Miller gown just for fun, stepped out of the dressing room to preen in front of the mirror and was met with the stares of every woman in the shop.

"That dress was made for you," one woman said.

"You're buying it," my sister declared.

The dress was perfect—a simple forties movie-star dress that was curvy in exactly the same places I was. I had absolutely nowhere to wear such a dress, but bought it and stuck it in the back of my closet for two years.

I made a split-second decision: I was going to wear the red dress. Because of its deep Vs, I couldn't wear a regular bra, but I thought, *Why wear one?*

I slipped the dress over my bare body and felt the cool glide of the satin lining fall from my shoulders to my ankles. I felt the fabric brush against my breasts. I pinned up my hair, put on some bright red lipstick and took off— to be the only woman wearing a colored dress in a room full of black and white.

I've never been a woman who turned heads. I have never felt confident enough in my looks to carry myself in such a way that I would. That night, however, I felt like the most beautiful woman in the world. I felt wholly alive in that red dress, and people must have picked up on the electricity, as if it were a fragrance. Men and women alike, people I knew and people I didn't know, came up to me to tell me how spectacular I looked, what a gorgeous dress I had on.

"You seem to glow," they said, and I loved the feeling of swishing around the room, feeling the weight of that dress as it draped to the floor, feeling it cool and clean on my bare breasts, which for that one last night, anyway, were still mine.

Many in that room were aware of my diagnosis and fear. The Sunday before, every hymn we sang in church made me cry, so I'd had to walk out of the service every ten minutes. But not one of my fellow parishioners mentioned my diagnosis the night of the party. It wasn't as if they were afraid or being sensitive or polite. It was as if my wearing the red dress prohibited the very idea of breast cancer, like a shield of armor.

A few days later, I got a call from the head of the party committee, thanking me for my help—which I'd abruptly stopped giving two weeks before. "We finally got everything cleaned up," she said, "and you were the hottest topic of discussion around the dish-drying rack."

"Me?" I said, thinking of the way church ladies chatter and gossip, and wondering what I could possibly have done.

"You were the most beautiful woman in the room that night, Jennie, and the most courageous. A lot of women in your shoes wouldn't have even shown up, let alone worn that dress."

Courageous? I thought. *Courageous?* So that was what courage felt like—that rush of judgment to know just what to do—or wear—that sense of satisfaction that nothing—not even cancer—was going to stand in the way of feeling utterly confident, that sweet perfume of feeling completely and totally alive. If that was courage, it suited me as well as the red dress.

I'd like to frame it.

Jennie Nash

Courage to Climb

*One's life shrinks or expands according to
one's courage.*

Anaïs Nin

What am I doing here? I ask myself as I stand on the edge of
the cliff, close my eyes, position my feet on the edge and
lean back into empty space. I take the first step backwards
over the edge, the ropes at once moving and supporting me.
Talking to myself alleviates fear, and I silently recite the
instructions: "Feet flat on rocks; pretend shoes have suction
cups; allow rope to slide through hands; feet shoulder-width
apart; don't forget, right hand pulled to hip is the brake." I'm
terrified and don't know if I can take another step.

Just weeks out of chemotherapy for a breast cancer
recurrence, I stand in the lobby of the Denver, Colorado,
downtown Holiday Inn, waiting for the Outward Bound
van that will transport the Challenging the Course of
Cancer group high into the Rockies. The recurrence has
left me shaken, and I need to throw myself back into life
and regain my courage.

Bus after bus arrives, loads and departs, and anxiety

increases as the lobby empties. Only a few people remain. We stare at one another for a moment and then converge to the center of the room. A young man about thirty looks at me questioningly and asks, "Challenging the Course of Cancer?"

"Yes," I reply, relieved to know I'm not alone.

"Emilio," he says and extends his hand. The others follow his lead, and we eagerly shake hands and exchange names.

At last the van arrives, and we begin the two-hour trip to the Outward Bound center near Leadville, Colorado. Excitement, apprehension, fear and hope emanate from these strangers, who reflect my own emotions. To succeed on this three-day adventure, we must learn to trust one another very quickly. Cancer is the only thing we presently have in common.

I'm balanced on the highest of several narrow steps that are nailed to a tree. Below, my companions stand in two rows, forming a human net with their arms. *Whoever thought of this exercise?* I ask myself as my body hugs the tree. I've just met these people—can I depend on them to keep my still fragile body from hitting the ground? They speak encouraging words, "Don't think about it; just let go. You didn't drop anyone when you were part of the net."

I close my eyes and breathe deeply—ten breaths, fifteen breaths. I lean back, free-falling safely into the human net.

The fear felt during the free-fall returns in the next exercise: rappelling. *Breathe,* I tell myself. My body relaxes, as do my lungs, and once again I lean out and back, allowing the rope to move me slowly downward. Just as I'm gaining confidence, I place my feet too closely together and swing to one side, almost losing control. I bring my feet to the rocks, stabilizing my swinging body. Though shaken, I feel an unexpected surge of excitement and energy. My feet make friends with the rocks; my body melts into the rope; I experience unencumbered freedom, rappelling for sixty feet.

Emilio and I are last in line for the rock climb; we adjust our harnesses and check our boots. Just as we're ready to begin, the rain comes, and all of us, nine participants and three counselors, huddle under a makeshift awning. Our bodies touch, and our breath mingles. The rain continues, and we laugh and talk as though we've always been friends. After almost an hour, John, one of the counselors, says, "We need to decide what to do." Emilio doesn't want to leave without climbing. Neither do I. It's his thirty-first birthday today, and climbing the rocks is his gift to himself.

He and I begin our climb—the ropes and rocks are wet and slippery. I'm fine for the first five or six feet, then the foot and handholds seem to disappear. I remind myself of the instructions: "Touch three places at all times. Don't use the knees." My legs aren't long enough to reach where I need to go, and I have to ignore the instructions and use my knees. I don't look down, only up. I see Lori, Tina and Jeff waiting for me at the top. They speak words of encouragement, and finally I'm close enough to reach up and take their hands.

During my solo night experience, I take inventory of what I've accomplished during the past two days. With flashlight balanced and listening to the music of night sounds, I record in my journal:

Trusted eleven strangers to catch me as I fell from a tree.
Rappelled down the cliffs and recovered without panicking when my body swung out of control.
Reached out to trust again and was not disappointed.
Came to understand that I'm brave.

Loaded with backpacks and sleeping bags, we begin the descent to the Outward Bound Center. We don't want this time to end, and we reluctantly follow the path through the trees, across a wooden bridge and along the creek.

Unexpectedly, Jeff turns off the path and leads us to a solid wooden structure nearly twenty feet high. We look at him questioningly. We thought the solo in the woods last night was the final challenge.

"This is the wall," he says solemnly. "You have forty-five minutes to get everyone, leaders included, up and over. No ropes or belts allowed, and no using the sides of the wall." He instructs us to put on our harnesses, then calmly walks away to talk with the other counselors. We're left to wonder whether anyone has ever completed this exercise.

After a few false starts, we begin to focus on the task. Emilio and Tina serve as ladders as we hoist Dana onto their shoulders. Extending as high as she can on her toes, she finally grasps the top board and pulls herself up and over the wall onto the narrow platform behind it. I'm next to climb the human ladder. Dana leans over the wall from the platform and grabs my extended wrists. I dangle in space as I attempt to swing my leg to the edge. At last, I swing high enough for Dana to release one of my hands, grab my leg and haul me over the top. One by one, my companions traverse the wall, until only Jeff and Emilio remain.

Emilio climbs on Jeff's shoulders and reaches for Tina's and Dana's extended hands. They grasp his hands, and he dangles as Jeff jumps and grabs his harness, unsuccessfully trying several times to climb up and over him. Jeff continues to slip, and we aren't certain he'll make it. We cheer him on, and gaining renewed energy, he at last pulls himself up and over Emilio, making it to the top.

Together, we hoist the hanging, stretched Emilio to the platform, finishing our task with five minutes to spare and with the invaluable knowledge that the only walls in life are those we construct ourselves—that cancer doesn't define who we are or determine what we can accomplish.

Michele V. Price

Abreast in a Dragon Boat

*I can't change the direction of the wind, but I can
adjust my sails to always reach my destination.*
Jimmy Dean

In the fall of 1994, I had surgery and radiation for what I
jokingly referred to as a "mild" case of breast cancer—
stage I. As a professor of physical therapy, I was acutely
aware of the risk of lymphedema, an irreversible, dreaded
swelling of the surgical-side arm. In fact, my own physical
therapist, who specializes in treating women with breast
cancer, chastised me for raking leaves one beautiful
autumn day.

"Repetitive upper body activities," she warned, "could
bring on lymphedema."

I started to read all I could about lymphedema, which
can be caused by lymph-node removal, radiation and obe-
sity, and I realized that even in the medical literature there
are a number of unverified assertions. Women are warned
never to carry a purse on their involved shoulder and to
avoid strenuous exercise with the affected arm for the rest
of their lives. For the rest of their lives! As a long-time

jogger and recreational soccer player, I was irked by the presumed need to avoid strenuous exercise.

Luckily, one of my colleagues at the University of British Columbia, Don McKenzie, M.D., Ph.D., a professor of sports medicine and exercise physiology, set out to challenge that myth. He organized twenty-four breast-cancer survivors into a dragon-boat racing team.

Dragon-boat racing is a competitive and recreational sport developed centuries ago in China. It involves eighteen to twenty paddlers who propel a forty to sixty foot wooden boat along a 500 to 650 meter course. It's a strenuous and repetitive upper body sport—just the type of exercise my physical therapist warned me against! (I took a certain mischievous pleasure in disobeying her orders, but you should always check with your doctor before undertaking an exercise program).

To prepare for on-water training, Dr. McKenzie and the other coaches developed a three-pronged, land-based training program, involving stretching exercises, three twenty to thirty minute aerobic workouts a week, and weightlifting to strengthen our upper arm and back muscles. I loved the training and the weekly regimen. I also loved my teammates—breast-cancer survivors all. Soon we developed friendships that endured both on and off the water.

Our team, Abreast in a Boat, has competed in dragon-boat festivals in Vancouver, Toronto, Seattle, Portland and Wellington, New Zealand, and it has fostered the formation of more than 100 other breast-cancer teams around the world. Not one of the original members has developed lymphedema, nor did the condition worsen for the two members who had pre-existing swelling. More significantly, many of the women from the team became important role models for me.

Three months after competing in New Zealand, I was

diagnosed with a second primary tumor in the opposite breast. Two of my teammates accompanied me to hear the worrisome initial diagnostic news from my surgeon: I had stage IIB. When I was deciding whether to have a bilateral mastectomy in June 1998, teammates who had been through the procedure bared their breasts (reconstructed and otherwise) to help me make my decision. During the dozen chemo sessions, at least one teammate was there with me, as a role model and supporter.

Although I had to sit out for my year of treatment and six months afterward, I began training and competing again in the spring of 2000. The women from my team, their partners and kids have become family to me. They have enriched my life in unexpected ways—inviting me to join their families for Christmas when I was too immune-compromised from chemo to fly home to my own, and serenading 150 guests at my fiftieth birthday party with songs they wrote about me and dragon-boat racing. I am so grateful for their ongoing love and support. After all, as one of my teammates said, "We're all in the same boat!"

Susan R. Harris
As previously appeared in
Mamm Magazine

Racing for the Cure

*It's all right to cry, but not for too long. I made
it, and so can you.*

Betty Ford

As a result of God's grace, the love and support of my
family and friends, and the skill of a talented team of doctors, I am about to celebrate my eleventh year of survivor-
ship. I fully expect to live to see my children graduate
from high school and college, get married, and have their
own children. I am overjoyed.

In 1995, my doctor said words I could hardly comprehend: "Mrs. Callahan, I am very sorry to tell you that you
have breast cancer." I was forty-two years old, with no history of breast cancer in my family. The pea-sized lump
that I found during a self-exam had not even shown up on
a mammogram.

I talked to my doctor for an hour, taking copious notes.
When the conversation was over, I was stunned to see
that I'd written down only a few words. I later realized
that she had explained the diagnosis over and over again,
but I just couldn't absorb the information. For days I held

the paper in my hand—not to read the scant information, but to hold the proof that cancer was really happening to me and I was not dreaming. I still have that piece of paper.

However, in June 1995, a month after surgery, my spirit was temporarily occupying that dark place between *hoping* that I would fully recover and *knowing* that I would. I decided to walk in the National Race for the Cure, which takes place every June in Washington, D.C.

My husband, two children and extended family joined me in the race. We drove to the nearest metro station. As we approached it, I noticed a stream of people walking toward the station entrance and was surprised the metro was so busy on an early Saturday morning. Moments later, I realized that all of these people were wearing Race for the Cure T-shirts. When we stepped into the subway car, race participants were sitting in every seat. Even though the station was on the outskirts of the subway line, there was standing room only. Most of the T-shirts were white (runner or walker), with a sprinkling of pink (survivors) and yellow (volunteers).

We exited the subway and walked toward the starting line on Constitution Avenue. As we cleared the tall buildings near the exit subway station, I was overwhelmed by the panoramic view of the starting line. There were 50,000 race participants that year. Nearly all were wearing "In Memory Of" or "In Celebration Of" placards on their backs. Somehow, I felt they were all there for me. My eyes wouldn't stop tearing.

Many racers were part of teams. There were teams from countries around the world, from corporations around the nation, and from schools around the Washington area. Each team carried a sign or a banner announcing its presence. There were Girl Scouts, military personnel, college students and babies in strollers. There were also the survivors, all proudly wearing pink—some robustly running at top speed, some being pushed in wheelchairs.

I happened to be assigned race number 409. During the race, the yellows were on the sidelines yelling, "Go 409!" and "Good going, 409!" I received high-fives from pinks, whites and yellows. When I finished the race, a loud speaker blasted to all 50,000 participants, "409 just crossed the finish line! Congratulations, 409!" I finished the race exhilarated with encouragement and hope.

After the race, my sister Maggie and I were chatting while waiting for the closing ceremony to begin. I saw my dear friend, Ginny, walk by with her family. She was also wearing pink—we had made our cancer journey together, and we greeted each other, laughing and crying. We were incredulous that we had bumped into each other in the midst of the tremendous crowd. When she walked away, Maggie and I saw the placard that she wore on her back. It said, "In Celebration of My Friend Ellen Callahan." Maggie and I hugged each other and cried.

I have participated in the race every year since 1995. Sometimes I wear pink, sometimes yellow, but I always cry. And Ginny and I somehow manage to find each other every year. Last year over 70,000 walkers, runners and volunteers came to the race. The race continues to nurture my hope and confidence in the future.

I am truly blessed.

Ellen Ann Callahan

This essay is dedicated to my courageous friend and fellow survivor, Ginny Westrick.

For Josie

We are not confused—we know we are two separate people—man and wife. Yet when we met, when we married, when we had children and grandchildren, we knew. Something existed between us, beyond us, that exists as a third entity—something each individual contributed to and could draw on.

And now we have cancer, knowing that one of us must fight an internal battle and one of us will tend the supply lines, knowing that the two of us are one, each afraid— each giving courage to the other, knowing we will endure.

1965—Sir Francis Drake High School, San Anselmo, California.

Third date, basketball game at Terra Linda, the path from the parking lot to the gym blocked by a wire cable: we duck under the wire, reaching for each other's hand to steady ourselves, knowing yet not knowing the meaning of holding hands, surprised by the electricity, delighted by the simplicity, content in the rightness of such a simple act.

And we never let go—even to arrange fingers in a more comfortable arrangement, not even to appease the dean of women and rules against public displays of affection.

We held hands to exchange rings, to deliver two

children, to teach them to cross the street, to make a swing for grandchildren, as we walked—one, two, three.

2001—Swedish Medical Center, Seattle, Washington.

Pre-op: I held her hand as she lay on the gurney waiting for Dr. Dawson. When he arrived, I let go of her hand and he took it in his and walked beside her, holding it.

Post-op: The doctor told me many things. I asked questions, relieved and worried. I wrote them down, looked for hidden meanings, sifted through hopes and fears.

He explained that she would be fine, detailed the required next steps. Information swirled, yet I knew his meaning fully and understood his gentle smile when he said, "I held her hand."

The Rapids: This turbulent river on which we travel is not of our choosing.

We were not heading in this direction when we slammed into the first rock. Cancer—malignant. It took three doctors before we could even believe we had hit a rock. By then, we were upside down, over the first falls, taking on water, spinning, gasping for breath.

When one is in a whirlpool, one cannot swim toward the surface, one cannot overcome the downward force of the water. One must swim downward with the pressure, letting the turbulence push down, out, then up. This requires presence of mind, especially when one is not sure what is up and what is down.

For the moment, we have righted the boat and are learning to paddle, know we are on the river, aware there is rough water still ahead, and there are people both on the bank and in the water to offer help and believe we will make it.

We will make this river our river.

Cancerland: We unfold the game board as one opens a fortune cookie hoping to discern the future. As much as we watch, cancer always makes the first move and catches us by surprise. We ask the experts: What are the rules? They tell of statistics, survival rates, possible outcomes, risks, but still, we must roll the dice, count out the spaces, slide into despair, climb upward in hope.

One must wait one's turn for treatment, must wait to learn the results of tests. Blood counts fluctuate. Side effects accumulate like so much debt. Must wait years to know for sure, years of worry and dread.

As children, we played simple games. Primary colors. Rewards came quickly, defeats forgotten easily.

As parents, we taught our children games to pass the time. Taught them to follow the rules: win or lose, we could always play again.

As grandparents, we understand the rules are unknowable, that time passes of its own accord, that this game is serious, and our best may not be good enough. Yet we start each day, stubborn, ready to compete.

As children on a bright day, we would hold a magnifying glass to catch the sun's rays, focusing the circle of light on a piece of paper into one point of intensity until the spot scorched, smoldered, flamed and burned.

Now machines focus unseen energy on those cancer cells that may have escaped the surgeon's dissection, the chemotherapy's poison.

Let there be light.

Let there be life.

Doug Manuel

No More Fear

*It is the knowledge of the genuine conditions of
our lives that we must draw our strength to live
and our reasons for living.*

Simone de Beauvoir

I've *always* been terrified of needles. I am one of those
people who faint at the sight of blood. All my life, every
time I had a shot or had blood drawn, I passed out in the
doctor's office—even when I went for my blood test to get
married. So I was *really* worried about all the needles I
would have to face during surgery and chemotherapy.

My sister Barbara and my husband, Don, came with me
to surgery. I had scheduled my same-day lumpectomy for
the first thing in the morning. I felt that if I was early, there
would be fewer chances of being pushed back by emer-
gencies and delays, and I would get to go home rather
than spend the night in the hospital.

All three of us were very nervous. It was 5:30 A.M., and
we hadn't eaten anything—me because I wasn't supposed
to, they because there hadn't been time. We arrived at the
reception area, courageous but sleepy.

The nurses took me in, and Barbara and Don were allowed to accompany me. I was settled into a small cubicle surrounded by medical equipment. A nurse came in to prepare me for the IV. I tried not to look at the long tube attached to the needle that she was preparing to insert in my arm.

Suddenly, Barbara said, "What about the numbing cream? I've heard you can put on something to make the area numb."

The nurse looked at her with surprise.

"Oh, we only give that to babies," she said.

"I'm a baby," I responded.

We all laughed a little, but she could see I was serious.

"Oh, all right. I'll be right back."

She returned a few minutes later and applied a white cream to my hand. She placed a clear tape bandage over it.

"It takes a few minutes to go to work. I'll be back."

I shot a triumphant look at my sister and Don.

"Thanks," I breathed a sigh of relief.

We three chatted for about ten minutes, talking about anything except the needles and my surgery. It really helped to have them there with me. I wasn't nervous now, and I felt completely loved and supported.

The nurse returned and inserted the IV into the large vein in the back of my hand. Thanks to the cream, I felt nothing. Absolutely nothing. A smile of shock and amazement lit up my face.

"How is that?" she asked.

"Fine, I can't even feel it. Thank you. Thank you so much!"

She smiled, "You know, that was a good idea. I don't know why we don't use it more often." I couldn't stop myself: I jumped up and gave her a hug.

"You will never know how much this meant to me. " I said.

She smiled, then stepped aside as the anesthesiologist came in, asked me if I was allergic to anything and hooked me up to the IV drip. Again, I didn't feel a thing. I smiled and waved to the angel nurse, my sister and my husband. I was wheeled away to the surgery room. My last thought was how loved I am, how kind the nurse was, and total amazement that I felt no fear.

I entered the Land of Needles with no fear. *That* is a miracle!

Mary Olsen Kelly

7
SURVIVAL

There is often in people to whom "the worst" has happened an almost transcendent freedom, for they have faced "the worst" and survived it.

Carol Pearson

"Even without lights, water or a roof,
this hurricane is a breeze compared
to surviving my breast cancer."

Fifty-One-Year Survivor!

Fifty-one years ago, when I was thirty-two, I discovered a lump in my left breast. It was "suspicious," and a radical mastectomy was performed with drains in the armpit, which needed daily care.

So began the "five-year cure" syndrome. If anything suspicious or questionable arose, I was carefully watched and hospitalized to undergo a battery of tests to see if there was any spreading of the cancer. What a happy day for all of us when the five-year period passed without complications! However, it was not so for some of my friends and acquaintances, so while I had reason to be grateful, thankful and jubilant, I had cause to wonder, WHY?

In 1965, thirteen years after the left mastectomy, small lumps began appearing in the right breast area. It was different from the first time, when I had only one lump. Once again, I waited six months—perhaps too long—before consenting to a radical mastectomy. But increasing pain had finally determined my choice: surgery (by the same surgeon) was undertaken, and the bone was scraped. This time I had no drains and no swelling, and once again began the five-year count. That was thirty-eight years ago, and I've had no recurrence.

I was certainly more fortunate than some other victims of malignancies, but I obliterated the "cancer" word from my vocabulary, referring to it by any other name I could substitute. Denial? Perhaps. But great faith, loving support of family, relatives and friends, and physicians and surgeons who provided exceptional care—all were comforting and provided great incentive to "overcome"!

Last year was my first experience with the Susan G. Komen Race for the Cure. My daughter told me that if I was able, I had to go and participate in the walk. The prior year was the first year she had done it, and she was so impressed with what she had seen.

I was reluctant. When I had my surgeries, people didn't talk about breast cancer. And if they did, it was in whispers. It was a dreaded disease, one that didn't have much hope of a cure, so I wasn't accustomed to talking about it, and that's why I had obliterated the word "cancer" from my vocabulary. There was not the widespread knowledge and support for breast cancer that I've learned exists today.

I didn't decide to go to the race until just a few days before the event, and I probably wouldn't have if my daughter hadn't refused to take "no" for an answer.

I was so impressed, as she had told me I would be, and I couldn't get over how many people were there and all that had been done to make the day special: the breakfasts, the volunteers, the sponsors. It was such a positive experience for me, I was amazed.

As I was putting the ribbons on my cap—all fifty of them!—more and more people approached me to ask me how many years it had been. When I said, "It has been fifty years," they couldn't believe it. I was hugged and kissed by strangers who felt a bond as I did. It allowed me to talk about something that I really hadn't been able to talk about for most of my life and, just as important, to feel as though I could provide some measure of comfort and support to those who were just experiencing what I had gone through many years before.

I appreciate all the work the foundation does to increase awareness of breast cancer. When you're struggling with cancer treatment and surgery, it's so important to be able to talk to others who understand or who have gone through the same thing. It's something that I didn't have in my day.

Last year, we had a small team that my daughter put together. This year we're trying to put together a bigger team. We told my husband and son about it, and they want to come, and I'm going to ask some of my friends to join us. How about you? Would you like to join along?

Kathryn O. Sharr

All the Gifts

The flight to Honolulu is a long one, and I lean my forehead against the cool, soothing window of the plane. I haven't been able to cry yet. The call came a few days ago; Mom has breast cancer and is going to have a mastectomy. I will be there for her, and I need to be there for me, too.

Plane time is strange time; you're in another place, and yet somehow you are nowhere. I let my thoughts wander to a time when I might lose her, not have her loving presence in my life and children who may never get to know her, and hot tears burn my cheeks. The morbid thoughts are shaken from my mind as the islands of Hawaii appear in the blue water below—it is beautiful and lush even from 10,000 feet, and my heart lightens.

The glorious aroma of Hawaii enfolds me as I leave the plane. My brother Jimmy places a plumeria lei around my shoulders. Common in Hawaii, this beautiful, fragrant gift from my mother is an appreciation of things done by hand, a gift of someone's time, a loving thought put into action.

Back at the house, Mom has made my favorite Hawaiian foods and lots of poi. She looks happy and relieved to see me.

The next day we see the surgeon. My mother seems to trust him and asks no questions. I like him, too, but ask many questions. He answers them all, and we feel that together we're making the right decision. Mastectomy has been the "gold standard" so far, in conjunction with adjunct chemotherapy. We talk about a lumpectomy, but my mother seems more secure with the mastectomy, so the decision is finalized.

A few days later we walk into the Queens Medical Center in downtown Honolulu. My brother and I are joking and teasing her to keep up all our spirits, but the gravity of the situation is etched on our faces. We dissolve into small talk to pass the time, the big talk too painful to say aloud.

I kiss her good-bye as she is wheeled into surgery and tell her, "I'll see you in a little while." I remind her to hurry up or Jimmy will eat her delicious hospital lunch. She doesn't laugh. I see fear creeping into her face—and sadness, too.

Three endless hours pass. Finally, the surgeon comes in and tells us everything went fine, and she is in recovery, able to see us. She opens her eyes and tears fall. "I didn't think it would hurt so much, Pamela; it's all pain." She squeezes her eyes shut.

Ten days later, we get the first full look at her scar. It is huge. It runs from the middle of her chest, around to her back, stopping just before her shoulder blade. It is red and angry, but the doctor says it will get better and starts to talk about reconstruction. Mom doesn't want to hear it.

"I'm too old and don't care how I look." She never has the reconstruction, partially because she doesn't want to have to worry about self-exams on the new breast. "I am happy to be alive; I will survive."

Survive she does. I make her a fake boob out of a Nerf ball and eventually convince her to buy a real prosthetic. Her ability to continue and thrive is amazing and inspiring to everyone who knows her.

Fast-forward eighteen years and my mother is still going strong at eighty-two. My sister asked her on her eightieth birthday how she keeps going. "I feel like that bunny with the drum. You know, I just keep on going."

She is visiting me in Connecticut, and I have a mammogram appointment. I'm running late as usual, and she waits in the car with my two boys, eight and twelve years old. They have their lunches and GameBoys, and since my appointments usually take no more than twenty minutes, I figure it will be fine as always.

In five minutes, I have my mammogram. "Wait a minute, the doctor will be right in to see you."

The technician comes back fifteen minutes later and says, "We need another close-up."

Now I'm waiting in another area; it's been forty minutes, and I'm worried about my kids and mother in the car—and about my boob. The radiologist comes in. "We need to do a sonogram; there is a shadow we can't quite make out."

After the sonogram, the doctor looks upset as I try to remain calm. What is bugging him is the fact that he can't *find* the shadow, whatever that is. They ask me to wait in another room. Then they hand me my X-rays and tell me, "Please call your gynecologist and have her recommend a surgeon."

I walk out to the car. My mother takes one look at me, and she knows.

Two weeks later, I'm at the hospital to deal with the lump. This means a surgical biopsy, and I'm being prepped. The only other time I've been in a hospital was to have babies, so it's bizarre to be in for any other reason.

My husband waits with me. "Small talk" again; "big talk" is too painful. Steve has always been there for me, his big blue eyes shining, not always saying anything, but always there. Our marriage is another one of life's gifts to me.

As I'm put on a gurney and wheeled away, he kisses me good-bye and says, "I'll see you later." The anesthesiologist puts something into my IV, and everything takes on a dream-like feel. I hear them talking, I hear scissors cutting thread, but it is all so far away. I find myself in the recovery room, no pain, slowly coming back to Earth. I go home and wait some more. Mom calls every day, but there is still no word. A few more days, and the biopsy is negative. It is a benign lymph node!

At my check-up I see my scar for the first time. It is angry and red, about an inch long, running on the same axis as my mother's. I have a tiny version of her scar, a tiny reminder of our connection. We are bound, my mother and me, by birth and family, by blood and pain, by humor and sorrow, by determination and survival, by love and spirit—all the gifts we share.

And we have the scars to prove it.

Pam Arciero

Dancing at Evan's Wedding

Health is the first and greatest of all blessings.
                                          Lord Chesterfield

In the fall of 1996, I was enjoying the good life . . . the mother of three young sons and happily married to a man I had loved and trusted since college. We lived in a beautiful home in a small Indiana town where I was a social and community leader and my husband a successful businessman.

I was a former *Seventeen* magazine model and a teacher at Plymouth High School. I was to receive a grant from the Lilly Foundation, recognizing my accomplishments as family and consumer services teacher. "They used to call it home ec," the woman said. By any name, it was a major accolade for my professional career and a proud moment.

It didn't last.

Fate was about to deal severe blows that would leave me personally devastated and fighting for my life. First, my husband of twenty-one years left me.

Five months later, I felt a tingling and drawing sensation in my right breast. I was knowledgeable about body changes; for ten years I had taught my students about breast and testicular cancer. The material was part of the curriculum, and though there is no history of breast cancer in my family, I had regular mammograms and faithfully did breast self-exams (BSEs). I didn't smoke or drink caffeine, only had a glass of wine occasionally, and took no drugs of any kind, except hormone replacement therapy. I was forty-three.

I had nursed my babies, which is a plus for women not to get breast cancer—besides that, it's the right thing to do, for many reasons. It had been a little more than a year since my last mammogram, and I had no reason to suspect anything. My doctor found nothing unusual at my appointment. A month later, I woke up to find extremely swollen lymph nodes in my right armpit . . . like a bunch of grapes. They weren't painful, but I knew something was seriously wrong.

I made an emergency appointment with the doctor; he ordered another mammogram immediately. It showed a small, definite change in breast tissue. A needle biopsy discovered a one-centimeter tumor that was infiltrating, so the surgeon removed four lymph glands for analysis.

All the tests were positive: a fast-growing malignant tumor, "worrisome and serious," according to the doctors. Four days later, I had a radical mastectomy and removal of eight of twelve nodes, also positive. Six months of chemo reduced me from a size twelve to a size six.

At first, when I started losing hair, I was brokenhearted. My youngest son, Evan, saw me crying and said, "Mommy, don't cry. Chas, Matt and I will take care of you." Then he went to the bedroom, got my wig out of the drawer and brought it to me.

"Put this on, Mommy. It'll make you feel better." And it did.

I lost the hair on my head and my eyebrows. As it began to fall out, I imagined that every follicle that died was now a dead cancer cell, so the balder I got, the more cancer was being destroyed. I shaved off the rest.

Evan went with me for my radiation treatments, an eighty-minute round trip. The doctors let him push the radiation buttons, and he believed he was truly helping me get well. I minimized the pain from the burn by holding on to one dream: I wanted desperately to dance at Evan's wedding—whenever that would be.

Nine months later, every method of testing for cancer proved negative, and six months later I underwent a seven-and-a-half-hour reconstructive surgery to form a new breast.

My dream of dancing at Evan's wedding is going to come true! I believe in angels, and, after all, I live on Angel Street, in Plymouth, Indiana.

Nancy Jaynes as told to Ida Chipman

Joy Is the Simplest Form of Gratitude

The joy of a spirit is the measure of its power.

Ninon de Lenclos

A person who has been diagnosed with breast cancer anxiously waits to celebrate the five-year mark. Many doctors will tell you, "After five years with no cancer recurrence, you are cured of breast cancer."

During those five years, your vocabulary may include words like biopsy, chemotherapy, radiation, tumor markers and tamoxifin. They are not just words—they are experiences.

During the first year you're busy fighting for your life. Your calendar has more doctor appointment pages than social events. You're still trying to accept the fact that your name has been used in the same sentence as cancer.

The second year, treatment is over, and your bald head now has peach fuzz. To a cancer patient there is no such thing as a bad-hair day: It is thrilling just to have hair, and it feels truly wonderful to have the wind blow through that new stuff on your head.

Years three and four, you start to relax. Every time you cough or have an ache or a pain, you no longer believe you might have a new cancer. Life is starting to become normal—you even visit the beauty salon to have your new hair styled.

The fifth year you graduate from the school of cancer. You've had a very tough teacher, but you did all your homework and learned your lessons well. A breast-cancer survivor never forgets the date she was told by her doctor that she has cancer. It is etched in her mind with all the other important events in her life. And graduation day, equally memorable, finally arrives after five long years of hard work. You stand a little taller, have a song in your heart and a wonderful smile on your face. It's a wonderful day! The pill box has been removed from the kitchen counter, and the wig has been pushed back to the corner of the closet, now accumulating dust.

No one wants to hear the word cancer once—and certainly never twice.

Three months after graduating from the school of breast cancer, a routine pap smear showed abnormal cells, and the doctor said, "It would be a good idea to have more medical tests done." I now learn more words: sonogram, CAT scan and that word biopsy again—and more blood tests. I had the tests and hoped I passed. The thought of having another cancer was unthinkable, and my mind repeated and repeated: *I've already paid my cancer dues.* I waited for the phone to ring, and when I heard my doctor's voice I hoped she was calling to do lunch.

Deep within my spirit I knew something was wrong . . . and heard that ugly word again. The demon of cancer had raised its head, and once more it had invaded my life. Now I was really angry! I had graduated from cancer school, and now I'd been sent back to first grade! I wanted to yell and scream! I needed to hit something, to release these demons!

The hard part is telling the people I love that I must have an extensive hysterectomy—more scars on my body. Oh well, my childbearing days are over, and my bikini days are long gone. Another trip to a hospital—just put the car on auto-pilot because it knows the way after so many journeys. I realize I need to approach this one as the last and live my favorite quote: "I might have cancer, but cancer does not have me." I will be the same positive person I was before.

After surgery I waited to hear if the words chemo and radiation would be spoken, but this time—this time—I heard the words: "No further treatment will be needed."

The wig can stay in the back of the closet, thank God! The pill box is back on the kitchen counter, but the color of the pills have changed. I am truly thankful that a routine pap test had shown there was a problem and a doctor ordered more tests. Twice I've been told I had cancer, and twice I have survived.

I see in the mirror a fun-loving, positive, upbeat woman, albeit scarred. I smile at her, and she smiles back. She knows she is a breast-cancer survivor!

Karen Theis

A Time to Listen

*True silence is a garden enclosed, where alone
the soul can meet its God.*

Catherine de Hueck Doherty

Standing in front of the kitchen sink, cleaning up yet another mountain of dishes, I complained loudly to myself. Here it was mid-December, and once again I wasn't nearly ready for the holidays at our house. I was failing miserably at a half-hearted attempt to make my oldest daughter's birthday cake before going off to work, and I'd have to leave early to be at school for a presentation my daughter was giving. Never enough hours in the day! Was I always going to be pulled in three different directions at once, doomed to play beat the clock? If only I could have time to read a book, watch a movie, be alone or just plain think. In less than two weeks, my prayers would be answered, and I would get everything I'd wished for—and more.

Wednesday, December 13, 2000, was another full day: a morning social obligation, mammogram at 10:30 A.M. and then school activities for the kids. I was dreading the whole day, especially the mammogram.

At the radiologist's office, I casually mentioned that during a self-exam I had noticed a small bump on my right breast. "Probably hormonal, no big deal," I told the technician. The area was marked and X-rayed. Strange, they called for an ultrasound—just trying to be thorough, I thought.

Then a doctor said, "You need to see a surgeon and have that taken out; there's a good possibility it's cancerous."

The next several minutes were a blur, but I do remember finding myself in the bathroom crying. *Wait a minute, I haven't even had the time to get this Christmas underway, and it might well be my last one. This can't possibly be happening to me. I'm only forty-six, in good health, exercise and go to church regularly, and have a young family to care for. Surely there has been a terrible mistake!*

At home there was a message from my gynecologist: "Call me!"

I did, and he offered me kindness, support and the name of a wonderful surgeon who saw me the very next day. I trusted him instantly. A biopsy confirmed it was malignant. The tumor was not very large, only five centimeters, and detected early. "You'll need another surgery," he said, "and radiation, but you can expect complete recovery."

The surgery could be done on Friday, three days before Christmas, or I could wait until after the holidays. I decided the sooner the better. How would we tell the kids, our family and friends? The children would have to be told first, since I would be going to the hospital before Christmas and staying overnight. At a family meeting during dinner, we simply told them the truth: "Mom has cancer."

Although the surgery was considered successful, a big surprise to all of us was that the tumor was almost twice the size as originally stated, and that both sentinel and axilliary lymph nodes were involved. This would change everything, and it meant there would be six rounds of chemotherapy followed by seven weeks of daily radiation. My immune system would be compromised. Work and vacation plans would have to be changed. I would lose my hair. All of a sudden, there would be plenty of time for me to read those books, watch that movie or just plain think. There would be many hours that would be spent alone recovering.

Although the scope of what was happening wouldn't occur to me for a while, God was answering my prayers in his own way. My life was beginning to change.

Looking for a positive spin, my daughters and I spent an afternoon wig shopping, the three of us trying on new colors and styles. I thought, *Well, this would be the first time in my life I would not have to worry about bad-hair days.*

I was in treatment from January through the end of August 2001. Most of that time was spent in a doctor's office, being examined, having blood drawn or getting daily injections. During that time I found time to watch only one movie and read two books. I slept quite a bit and certainly had plenty of time to think, but most of my time was spent listening . . . listening to others tell their stories, celebrating with other patients who were well enough to go on a long-awaited vacation, giving hugs and good wishes to those who had finished treatment and always marveling at the patience, skill and kindness of the oncology nurses, appreciating the brilliance of my oncologist and surgeon.

I participated in seminars, workshops and clinics, watched the seasons change, listened to my kids laugh, had actual conversations with my husband, learned how to draw eyebrows on my pale face, became close friends with a certain baseball hat, but best of all came the startling realization that the life I have, although sometimes crazy, was a good one and certainly one I was not ready to abandon.

Cards, letters and well-wishes arrived often. I've kept every one of them and will always be touched by the time taken by all of these people, some of whom I barely knew, to lift my spirits and send encouragement and support my way. On those especially bad days, I would take them out and read them again and again. They provided a renewed energy and determination to be strong and fight hard.

My diagnosis was over two years ago. There are still days when I'm tired, cross and angry, and don't think I can fit it all in, but I'm very pleased to still be here to fit in what I can. God's gift to me was to listen to my prayers and answer them in a way that would allow me to realize how truly lucky I am to have a loving husband, three beautiful children and wonderful friends. I'm still busy, but never too busy to take time for an impromptu lunch, a cup of coffee, take a walk or listen to a friend. Now when I find myself standing in front of the kitchen sink, cleaning up those mountains of dishes, I smile and thank God for the second chance to truly enjoy the life he has given me.

Donna Andres

The Olsen Girls

Light tomorrow with today.

Elizabeth Barrett Browning

My little sister turned fifty today—the one I carried around when she was a one-year-old and I was two and a half. I told everyone, "My baby. This is my baby."

She had a naturally curly, blonde ponytail and big blue eyes. "Oh, she looks like a princess," strangers would exclaim. My brown eyes downcast, I nodded, brown hair bobbing.

Always calm and observant, she would sit in the middle of the living room, serene and quiet as I ran around the room, a four-and-a-half-year-old doing cartwheels, turning somersaults, singing show tunes, kicking up my heels—anything to get attention and applause. At three years old, she already knew she was loved. She was enough and didn't have to work for it.

She had a pretty singing voice, though she didn't think so. I taught her songs so we could sing harmony. We put on shows in the garage, big productions with makeup and costumes gleaned from my mother's cast-offs. In the backyard we would perform acrobatic feats of wonder using the garden hose and creating a circus for all the neighborhood kids. We were a team—we were sisters.

We discovered books together and became bookworms, each checking out fourteen books a week from the local library, and reading all twenty-eight before they were returned and exchanged for a new tower of fourteen each. We worked through *Mary Poppins*, *Little Women*, Jack London and all the *Oz* books, the *Shoes* books (*Ballet Shoes*, *Skating Shoes*, etc.), and *A Wrinkle in Time*. We loved fantasy and stories about girls who were heroes.

Neither one of us was popular in high school; we were both smart and fell into the geeks and hippies segment of the teenage caste system. Bored with normal activities, we opened our own fashion boutique at fifteen and thirteen, designed and sewed all our own clothes, and with the help of our friends we filled a whole store with our creations. We even made costumes for rock groups.

College for me, Europe for her, then we came together again in the early seventies to open a bikini shop in Maui. We could do anything—we were sisters and a team.

Relationships and marriages followed, years of working in the theater for me, years of working in publishing for her. We were always connected, always close.

Then I was diagnosed with breast cancer three years ago, and she dropped everything to come and be with me. She cooked hundreds of meals and froze them, cleaned our house top to bottom, and went with me to scary chemotherapy treatments. At forty-eight years old, I finally learned what she had always known—I was loved; I was enough; I didn't have to work for it.

I'm fine now, and she and I talk every week from 3,000 miles away. We're a deeply connected team, and our husbands joke about how lucky they are to have married the

Olsen Sisters.

How could she be fifty? How could I be almost fifty-two? Well, that's the magic. She is really still my baby, and we're still singing songs together, putting on puppet shows in the garage, reading books and now traveling the world. Every time I think of her, whether we are together or apart, we are all these things. She has been there with me, through all of it. We know all the secrets . . . we were there. *Together.*

I threw a big party for her fiftieth birthday. Everyone was asked to bring a skit or poem or song. We learned the song "Sisters" from *White Christmas* and performed it at the party; at the end, the crowd applauded and someone yelled, "Do it again. We want to hear it again!" So we did. And I'm sure we'll do it again and again over the next fifty years. The Olsen Girls never quit. We're a team, forever and ever. We're survivors. We're sisters.

Mary Olsen Kelly

Laughter Is Bubbly!

Against the assault of laughter nothing can stand.

Mark Twain

One sunny afternoon about two or three months after I had finished chemotherapy and radiation, I was outside watching my husband, Walter, wash our car. I decided to help.

He really didn't want me to because I was still very weak and tired from the treatments for breast cancer, but being very persistent (translation: stubborn), I insisted. He finally agreed and brought a little stool for me to sit on and said I could wash the tires. I did this for a while, but it was very awkward sitting and scrubbing around the spokes in the wheel cover, so I stood up and leaned over.

My prosthesis popped out of my bra, fell in the soapy water and slid right under the car. We couldn't see it in all the bubbles, and Walter was afraid to move the car for fear of running over it. So I slid under the car and fumbled around and finally found it. Retrieval was difficult because it was so slippery in the soapy water, but I finally had it in hand and plopped it right back where it belonged, bubbles and all.

I've always wondered how many people witnessed that spectacle. You see, I forgot to mention that we live on the busiest street in our town.

We laugh a lot at our house—always have. Laughter is indeed the best medicine!

Judy Averitt Hayes

Bad news, people. The latest research indicated that laughter really is the best medicine.

Diagnosis: Canceritis

Trouble is only opportunity in work clothes.

Henry J. Kaiser

It was just a little bump. A little red mosquito-bite-looking bump on my stomach, discovered while I was taking a shower.

I have skin tags, moles, beauty marks, age spots and other "skin decorations" too insignificant to have names, but I'd never had one on my stomach. I didn't think about it again . . . until the next day. Again in the shower, I noticed the little red bump and then forgot about it once I turned off the water.

On day three, when the bump hadn't gone away, I started getting nervous. I found myself surreptitiously lifting my shirt throughout the next couple of days to check it, and each time it was still there. I became more alarmed and tried to stay calm, but my heart skipped a beat.

I lived in a steadily increasing state of panic for seven long days and then did what any woman who had just finished breast-cancer treatment would do: I got to my doctor's office as fast as I could!

When I had been diagnosed with breast cancer, I immediately thought I was going to die. But as the days and weeks passed, I realized I just might be one of the lucky ones who made it and began to relax a little.

By that time, I was fully engaged in my treatment plan and doing everything possible to be well again. I tried to cover all the bases: combining conventional medicine's chemo, surgery and radiation with not-so-conventional treatments like meditation, visualization and dance movement therapy. I became an expert in my kind of breast cancer and drove my oncologist crazy with questions about bizarre therapies I'd found on dubious Web sites. I felt like I had a handle on this cancer thing . . . some control.

After nine months of total immersion in medical appointments, procedures and theories, focused only on my healing, I finished treatment. Wow! I was ecstatic and relieved that I had survived all the poking and prodding and probing and plotting. I thought, *Now my life can get back to normal—no more treatments or doctor appointments or tests!*

The euphoria of completing treatment lasted one week. Then it hit me that I was no longer doing anything to keep the cancer away. I felt like a tightrope walker performing without a net.

I became obsessed with checking for signs that *it* was back. Breast self-exams were not enough: I performed total body exams. Cysts I'd had for decades became suspect. Moles that had been part of my physical landscape from birth were examined daily for changes. Showers became agonizing events as I scrutinized every inch of my body for evidence that *it* had taken over again. I had a full-blown, hard-core case of CANCERITIS.

Yes, canceritis—the most common and least treatable long-term side-effect of breast cancer. Shortly after my diagnosis, on the phone with my mother, a forty-five-year survivor, she was telling me how funny her surgeon had been years ago when she'd gone through her breast-cancer experience. She laughed as she recalled one visit. After listing all her aches and pains that proved the cancer had returned, he asked: "Where did you receive your medical degree?" I remember rolling my eyes and thinking how incredibly paranoid she was.

So, a few months later, here I was doing the same thing over a little red bump! And I wasn't the only one: I'd met many women who had survived breast cancer, and every one of them had canceritis. Some called their doctors daily with "symptoms," some just thought about calling, but all of them were preternaturally aware of every nuance of their bodies. And their "symptoms" had begun shortly after their treatment had ended.

Hair grows back, nausea goes away—the body heals. But the mind gnaws on that cancer thing like a dog gnaws on a bone—compulsively for a time, and then burying it, digging it up, burying it, digging—again and again. There are many medications and therapies to heal the body's wounds, but only one treatment for the mind. The magic bullet for alleviating the symptoms of canceritis is time. And the more time that passes, the less canceritis you have. My mother is cured of it, forty-five years later.

However, it had been only forty-five days for me when I found that little red bump on my stomach, and so the possibility that the cancer had come back was pretty much number one on my list of "what it could be." The doctor said it was nothing. I asked how she knew it was nothing. She said it didn't look like cancer, didn't feel like cancer, wasn't in a logical place for cancer to be. I repeated my question. She explained that just because I've had cancer doesn't mean I'm not a candidate for other illnesses and conditions (hardly fair, if you ask me). And I said that sounded reasonable, but how did she know it was nothing?

Just to get rid of me, she sent me to the dermatologist—who told me it was nothing. I asked how she knew it was nothing. She said it didn't look like cancer, didn't feel like cancer, wasn't in a logical place for cancer to be. I repeated my question. Just to get rid of me, I think, she removed that little red bump, did a biopsy of it and proved that it was indeed nothing.

I felt a lot better without that little red bump on my stomach (of course, now there's a little red scar instead), but I realized how foolish I'd been. It's understandable that I would immediately suspect cancer, and it was responsible of me to consult a doctor, but I did go a little overboard, insisting on a second opinion and a biopsy. That canceritis definitely had me going.

So I've decided to take a lesson from my mother and think twice before diagnosing myself with cancer every time I have a little ache—or a little red bump. And I've decided to stop the anatomical examinations in the shower every day. Why go looking for trouble? Why live the rest of your life worrying about every little something that pops up?

And I plan on making those changes just as soon as I get back from the doctor. You see, I've got this odd pain in my finger and . . .

Lori Misicka

8

GRATITUDE

There shall be eternal summer in the grateful heart.

Celia Thaxter

The Twelve Gifts of Chemo

*I always feel that the great high privilege, relief
and comfort of friendship was that one had to
explain nothing.*

                                        Katherine Mansfield

When I was diagnosed with breast cancer, I was flooded
with love and support from a wide circle of friends. Cards,
flowers, phone messages, e-mails and meals all were dearly
appreciated and helped me have some bright spots during
those most unsettling of times. But the efforts of one special
friend really stood out.

When I was told I should undergo twelve weeks of
chemo resulting in "100 percent hair loss," I never
dreamed I would actually look forward to my "chemo
days." Of course, I knew I would look forward to them in
the sense that having chemo would reduce my chances of
a recurrence, but actually looking forward to the days
with anticipation and excitement never occurred to me . . .
until my dear friend Chris worked her magic. She had
already begun to do all the dear and loving things an
extraordinary friend would do, such as acting as my

"communications director" and gatekeeper, organizing a weekly delivery of meals, filling my bedroom with ten vases of flowers to welcome me home from my first surgery, doing research and helping to care for my three young children so my husband could be with me.

And then the day of my first chemo treatment arrived. Chris showed up at my doorstep, as she would every week for twelve weeks, with the first of her gifts for "The Twelve Weeks of Chemo," delivered to the tune of "The Twelve Days of Christmas." The first week was "A Travelogue and Some Tea" (a very funny travel book by Bill Bryson titled *Tales from a Small Island*), accompanied by a card Chris had designed herself, which clearly took an enormous amount of time. Even though the card said "On the First Week of Chemo, My Girlfriend Gave to Me . . . A Travelogue and Some Tea," I didn't catch on that this was to be an every-week deal. However, after week two, when Chris again showed up with a card saying "On the Second Week of Chemo, My Girlfriend Gave to Me . . . Two Turtle Doves" (two Turtle candies and two Dove Bar candies), I started to get it, and so did my husband and children. When week three rolled around, I was excited to receive my surprise, and the first thing the children asked when they got home from school was, "What did Mrs. Helmholz bring?" By week four, it was one of the first questions my chemo nurses asked, and I started bringing in my treasures to show them. Chris had managed to find loving ways for our family look to forward to each week. My chemo nurses even looked up and printed the words to the song because none of us could quite remember what weeks seven and beyond were, and we were trying to guess what would come next. (It turns out that Chris had used this same technique, but the Web site she consulted had the wrong order of things, which caused her great consternation, but made me giggle all the more.) Here is the complete list of her weekly gifts:

First Week: "A Travelogue and Some Tea."

Second Week: "Two Turtle Doves."

Third Week: "Three French Hens"—a box découpaged with three chickens and filled with Snickers bars.

Fourth Week: "Four Caring Words"—a homemade pillow with the words "Strength," "Friends," "Love" and "Family."

Fifth Week: "Five Gold Rings"—five gold wine charms.

Sixth Week: "Six Things Worth Saying"—a beautiful framed copper and metal art piece with the words "Go for it," "Enjoy life," "Expect miracles," "Why not," "Simplify everything" and "Dream big" engraved on metal touch stones/coins.

Seventh Week: "Seven Swans A-Swimming"—a stitched art piece with seven matronly women in swim suits (which Chris promised did not resemble us!).

Eighth Week: "Eight Malts a Milking"—a lovely basket filled with eight packages of malt balls.

Ninth Week: "Nine Crumbcakes Crumbling"—nine homemade, delicious crumbcakes.

Tenth Week: "Ten Pipers Piping"—a small bowl with ten copper pipes artfully attached to a water pump to create an original water fountain.

Eleventh Week: "Eleven Flames a Dancing"—an elegant votive stand with eleven candles arranged vertically.

Twelfth Week: "Twelve Tins A-Keeping"—a magnetic board with twelve magnetic tins with lids attached. The lids were decorated with pictures of my children.

For the twelfth and final chemo treatment, in addition to "Twelve Tins A-Keeping," Chris made me a "courage doll" using wire and fibers from a piece of Tibetan prayer cloth she had long treasured. Her note said,

This doll represents courage and strength. It represents you. The fibers are strong and beautiful. They

protectively wrap the form, yet leave room for growth.
The wire gives it shape, yet it is flexible when needed.
The doll is wrapped in a piece of the prayer cloth to
remind you that you are not alone and will always be in
my prayers.

As if all this weren't enough to let me know I was loved and supported, when I had to have a mastectomy following chemo, Chris made me my own personal voodoo doll complete with pins.

Wandering around my house, nearly a year since my diagnosis and six months since my last treatment, everywhere I see signs of Chris's support. How much love and time must she have spent thinking, creating, designing and delivering—all to make me feel her friendship.

Many say you learn a lot about your true friends when you go through an experience like this, but I think it's slightly different. I don't believe it's a "test" of friendship—I believe that all my friends are true friends who happen to show their support in different ways. What I learned is really two-fold: first, the capacity for love in this world is immense; second, there are some extraordinary souls who, like Chris, have an amazing gift to give and are so generous of nature, but so shy of praise, that they are only truly appreciated in times of trouble. I don't think I have yet been able to convey to Chris how truly healing all her thoughtful gifts were, how they touched my heart to the core and gave me strength. One of our mutual friends had worried that her humorous approach might not be appropriate, but Chris knew how important laughter and love are to healing and coping, and she found just the right mix to help me feel cared for, but not smothered; honored but not pitied; lifted up but not carried.

Sally Fouché

My Life

If I could live my life over,
I'd do some things differently.
I'd play more, laugh more and love more,
And allow myself to be free.

I'd do more to and for others
As I'd like done to and for me.
I'd forgive myself more often,
I'd give more and do more freely.

I'd practice more relaxation,
Listen to what the body says.
I'd smell more flowers, see more trees,
Include more nature in my days.

I'd worry less about neatness
And how other people see me.
I'd ease up far more on strictness
And live life spontaneously.
I'd thank people far more often
And thank God for all that is me.
I can't live my life all over,
So I'll be the most I can be.

Kathy Chamberlin

Payback Time

Joy can be real only if people look upon their life as a service and have a definite object in life outside themselves and their personal happiness.

Leo Tolstoy

When I was told I had breast cancer, I never dreamed I would live long enough to write about it thirty-six years later. In my case, my doctor wasn't optimistic even if I had a mastectomy. The news was devastating, of course. I was forty-three and still had a lot of living to do. How could I handle it? How would my friends and family handle it? Should I even tell anyone? And if I did, could I tolerate their uncomfortable expressions of sympathy and clumsy attempts to comfort me with words like, "I know you'll be just fine"?

And every time I saw people whispering, I was sure they were whispering about "poor Lee." For one year, five years or whatever time I had left, I did not want to spend it being pathetic! I never needed sympathy before. I was raised with love, humor and optimism in an upper-middle-class family, and was fortunate enough to have two careers of my own choosing. In the first, the music business, I was an advance publicist and agent for name bands such as Tommy Dorsey and Ray Anthony. My second career was in advertising.

Now I was challenged to put my creative skills to work in the most important campaign of my life. I realized it was up to me, and only me, to set the stage so everyone could be at relative ease with my situation. I knew that moods are contagious. By conveying that I was optimistic and upbeat, my attitude could permeate to those around me. It worked. No longer did people tiptoe around the subject of my surgery.

After my mastectomy, I recovered quickly and actually went to a Falcons/Steelers football game six days after surgery, then to work the day after that. The more I came back to the real world after the "worry world," the more I realized I had a debt to pay for my life.

I made sure I had regular mammograms, and five years later I needed another mastectomy. The test had caught the problem early, and my prognosis was excellent.

I contacted our local American Cancer Society (ACS) to find out how I could help. They suggested I go door-to-door in my apartment building to solicit contributions. I discovered that the previous year the "grand" sum of twenty-seven dollars was collected from 120 apartments. Certainly, there had to be a more fruitful way!

By the grace of God and a few glasses of wine with friends, I was able to think of a much better way to raise money for the ACS. I went door-to-door inviting my neighbors to a cocktail party at my apartment. The minimum contribution was five dollars. I added, "I'll gladly accept more."

Result: $325 and the beginning of my thirty-six years of benefits for the American Cancer Society. It was also the beginning of neighborhood parties throughout Atlanta—

and, eventually, Georgia—these replaced the time-worn, ineffective door-to-door solicitations.

After the first year, I moved to a larger condominium complex, and the parties grew. After the fourteenth year, they had gotten so large that I had to have them at the complex clubhouse that could accommodate the 300 or more people who attended.

Among the hors d'oeuvres I made for my first party were meatballs. Everyone loved them, so they became a tradition, and I considered them a good-luck omen. The first year I made one hundred meatballs, but as the parties grew, so did the number of balls. The following years, making them became a party unto itself. My friends would gather around the dining-room table where I had placed a thirty-pound mixture of raw meat and seasonings. As they rolled and rolled, I cooked and cooked up to 1,000 meatballs! My friends ended up with soft hands from the fat in the meat, and I ended up splattered. We had a great time!

The other food and liquor were donated. Local sports celebrities volunteered as bartenders. Musicians and entertainers offered their talents freely, and all expenses were kept to a minimum. By then, the minimum donation had grown to twenty-five dollars (I would still accept more), and everyone thought it a great bargain. The word went around Atlanta, "It's the best deal in town . . . and the most fun!"

The affair was no longer just a neighborhood party. The crowd was well-diversified and included senators, members of Congress, and our mayor—who all showed up in election years!

After twenty-eight years of "partying" and $291,000 in Atlanta for the American Cancer Society, I moved to St. Simons Island, Georgia, where I am volunteer chairman of neighborhood parties in our county. During the eight years I've lived here, my parties alone have raised approximately $85,000.

Sometimes I sit back and reflect how different things would have been had I not had cancer. Well ... the Cancer Society would have missed more than $376,000, and I would have missed all those wonderful parties and the generous people who attended them.

But most of all, I would have missed the deep appreciation of simply being alive.

Lee Scheinman

You're Gonna Eat That?

I feel like I'm fighting a battle when I didn't start a war.

Dolly Parton

In case you're wondering where to hook up with a bunch of breast cancer survivors, you may find them in the natural-foods section of the supermarket, scouring labels for traces of soy.

Like beauty queens who are expected to uphold the standards of the pageant as they travel the world on their goodwill tours, breast-cancer survivors are often expected to be paragons of healthy eating. I flinched before bacon and smoked meats for a long time after my diagnosis, muttering such things as "unclean!" and pulling my shawl tighter around my face like a vampire at the first streaks of dawn.

In fact, one of the first things I did while under the influence of the steroids I got along with chemo was to throw out everything in my kitchen. "I don't know what poisoned me, but I'm getting rid of it!" I said in my steroid-induced, three A.M. frenzy. Never mind that breast cancer can strike even if you're mainlining phytoestrogens; I had to blame something, and closest at hand were frying pans encrusted with what I believed to be carcinogenic evidence. I admit now it is much more likely that I simply wanted to justify a spending spree at Williams-Sonoma.

Breast-cancer survivors are attracted to the idea of impeccable eating habits mainly because we feel betrayed by our bodies. But there's pressure on us from other sources as well, thanks to that famous study of Japanese women who, when they moved to Hawaii and changed their diet to a fast-food American one, developed a higher incidence of breast cancer. We still don't know precisely what in an American diet produced this effect (although I'd put my money on "supersizing"), and we don't know for sure precisely what about their former diets may have protected the women. Although everyone assumes it's soy, I'm hopeful it's the tempura.

The initial rush to culinary perfection can be very heady. For six months, I was a vegan, which is a vegetarian who doesn't eat . . . well, who doesn't eat anything. No meat, fish, eggs, dairy—just a lot of tofu pies disguised as chicken and visits to a particular restaurant where everything on the menu was in quotes, like "cheeseburger" or "BLT."

Being a vegan was not onerous for the time I was devoted to it. What was more annoying than a life without cheese was when I went back to normal eating and other people looked at me like, "You had breast cancer, and you're gonna eat THAT?" Just as politicians are expected to be monogamous and movie stars are expected to roll out of bed perfectly beautiful, breast-cancer survivors are expected to set a culinary example. And the people criticizing us are often the ones with steak juice running down their chins.

I think it's because they've displaced their own fears on us about getting cancer. Everyone wants a talisman to

ward off disease, and just as it was easier to blame my cancer on my kitchen equipment or eating habits, people are
comforted to think we can control our fates through
healthy eating.

Unfortunately, vegetarians get breast cancer, too, so
this theory is not without its holes. But human nature per-
sists. The next time you order something doused in butter
and someone gives you the evil eye, tell them to go sit on
a rice cake and mind their own business. Even beauty
queens only have to serve for a year. Then they get to live
the way they want, with or without a tiara always on their
heads like a halo.

Jami Bernard
As previously appeared in
Mamm Magazine

Another Kind of Miracle

Avoiding danger is no safer in the long run than outright exposure. The fearful are caught as often as the bold.

Helen Keller

It was a beautiful, clear spring day when Laura, my best friend for the last ten years, called to say she was dying. "The doctors say it's in my brain now, and it won't take much longer."

Thirty-seven years old, the mother of two young children, and the doctors were right. She died the following November.

"It wasn't supposed to turn out this way!" I shouted at God. "Laura should have had a miracle. Damn it, she deserved a miracle."

She was first diagnosed with breast cancer at thirty-two, a shockingly young age for such a vicious disease. The younger you are, the more virulent the cancer. When Laura first told me her news, I, being a published writer, sat down to write an inspirational novel for her.

In my novel, she was a character who'd had cancer

many years before, a strong and resilient woman who'd beaten the odds and survived.

Although I may still finish that novel even though Laura didn't make it, I soon put the novel aside and embarked on a more practical plan. Along with Jamie Miller, another friend of Laura's, I began to work on collecting stories of Christmas miracles. Not only would a collection of Christmas miracle tales find an audience, I thought, but it would also bring in some money for Laura and her husband.

Jamie and I interviewed many people who had experienced miracles at Christmastime, and then we wrote up their stories. Laura kept track of the administrative end of the project, and we produced a book for William Morrow, *Christmas Miracles: Magical True Stories of Modern Day Miracles,* that became a national bestseller.

How wonderful it was to be able to spread the word about the incredible things that can happen when we open our hearts and believe. Interview after interview convinced me miracles are everywhere, if you just open your eyes to the mystery of life.

I had a secret goal during the miracle book project. I believed with all my heart that if Laura was involved in this miracle project, if she lived and breathed the idea of miracles day in and day out, if she helped to spread the word that miracles can and do happen, then she, too, would be given a miracle. The hand of God was everywhere in these tales. We believed that same hand would reach down to allow her to stay with her children, to be the mother they needed her to be.

Our one Christmas book turned into a series of five books on miracles. But all the while, as our books grew more popular and we gathered more tales of miracles, Laura grew sicker. Five years after she was first diagnosed, she died.

In the months following Laura's death, I was furious with God. Why, after all of the good that she had done in her life, did God allow her to die? Why didn't she get her miracle?

The answer came to me on another clear spring morning, an eerie twin to the day that Laura had called with her devastating news the year before. As I looked out my office window at the blooming azaleas, the astra lilies hanging heavy from the weight of their flowers, I suddenly realized that there had been a miracle for Laura after all: I hadn't noticed the miracle of the last few years because it wasn't the one I wanted.

I wanted Laura to live. That was what I was asking from God, and anything less was unacceptable. But God knew all along that Laura would die, so God gave her the miracle she would need. She would need help with her children, so he gave her a circle of friends who would pitch in. She and her husband would need help with their finances, so he sent the miracle books project and allowed her to earn an income that would not require her to spend time away from her children in her final years of life. She would not live long, so he gave her a way to have an impact far greater than most people have in their first three decades. Her name will live on in her books, and even after her death she will continue to inspire others in their time of need.

God gave her the miracle she needed, even if it wasn't the one I wanted. I am grateful that I finally saw it.

Jennifer Basye Sander

The Snapshot

A wonderful snapshot was taken during the 1998 Pittsburgh Race for the Cure. The picture speaks of all the raw emotions felt by survivors who participated. There is sadness and joy that only we survivors understand. I was in the picture, and it has been used for publicity for the race. The funny part of the whole story is that the only thing you see of me is the back of my head. The person I was embracing was never recognized. They were able to contact me because my name was on my back.

The person who originally contacted me about the picture has made an impact on my life, and I will be forever grateful to her. She kept telling me that I had a story to tell and that others needed to hear it. My story has now been told in a TV documentary, the snapshot has appeared on the cover of a magazine, and I have done public speaking engagements. None of this would have been possible if it had not been "meant to be." The picture didn't reveal my face, but it gave me a voice.

For five years I tried to find the person I was embracing in the picture. Every year I went to the race searching for this woman in the crowd of thousands, hoping to recognize her. Every year that went by I started to think that perhaps she didn't make it. This is a part of the reality we live with every day as a survivor.

I got my invitation to a luncheon held annually in Pittsburgh for survivors and went alone, feeling a little awkward. I wasn't alone for long; I met two of the nicest ladies who invited me to sit with them.

This is where fate and "meant to be" come into the picture: They asked me to go ahead into the room where the presentation would be and save them each a seat. I had to find a row that had three empty seats. They soon joined me, and we held hands crying during the song, "We Share a Bond." The person in front of me began to cry, and I noticed there was no one sitting on either side of her. I felt a great need to give her a hug, and I did so from behind. Without turning around, she gently patted my hand that rested on her shoulder and thanked me.

As the program was ending, the lady turned around and thanked me, saying, "You must have known I really needed that."

I couldn't believe my eyes. I asked, "Have you been at any of the past races? You look so familiar."

She replied, "Maybe you saw me on the cover of the magazine they put in the race packets. I'm the one being hugged."

I burst into tears and said, "I've been searching for you for five long years!"

I've had so many wonderful things happen to me since I was diagnosed with breast cancer, and sometimes I need reminding of how bad it really was. I am a twelve-year survivor now, and the years have been an awakening. The people I've met along my "detour" have led me to places I would not have otherwise gone. I believe more than ever that I am here for a reason.

Elaine Zalar

"Thanks for your support, ladies. I never knew
such loss could lead to such a find."

My Guardian Angel

Grow old with me; the best is yet to be.

Robert Browning

I have always been a very modest person and always will be.

The nurse told me, "You can get up and go to the bathroom on your own now." Doug, my husband, was there to help me get up and out of bed, my right arm dangling loosely and chest wrapped tightly following my mastectomy. I felt like a mummy on one side.

I decided I could go it alone and moved forward to the bathroom, very embarrassed because my rear end was flashing.

I said, "Honey, don't you say a word."

He did. "Sweetie, I like that gown so much, maybe we can find you another one at the store when you get out of here."

With my humor back in place, I replied, "Well, if we're really lucky, maybe they will leave my fanny alone for now."

We both hee-hawed, and that's the way we continued to handle the situation.

When we did go home, I must admit I had a hard time allowing him to help me with my bandage, but, of course, it was not something I could do for myself. As he gently bent over me, the tears were rolling down my face, and he did the most astonishing thing: he leaned down, kissed my bandage and said, "Nanci, I am so thankful for that scar! Every time I look at it, I thank God, because if you didn't have it, I would have lost you. So there is no reason for us to feel anything but praise to God for the surgery. It has saved your life."

I believe that God, knowing the adversity that has been in my life way before my marriage and since, sent a special man to me. It wouldn't surprise me one bit if my husband is also my very own guardian angel. I'm thankful for him every day. Through seventeen years as a survivor and forty-seven years of marriage, we are still thanking God for the surgery and for each day, one day at a time.

Nanci L. Stroupe

Hearts and Flowers

I've been no more than a medium, as it were.

Henri Matisse

It was June 1988, and my husband was speaking on the phone with my surgeon's nurse. My mother was with me as my husband confirmed that the breast cancer I had survived six years before had returned.

I had noticed a change in the appearance of my breast. Aware that this was a sign of breast cancer and knowing how important early detection is, I immediately made an appointment with my surgeon. After several tests and confirmation that the cancer had returned, my doctor recommended removal of my right breast and six months of chemotherapy.

I was frightened beyond belief and numbed. I couldn't believe this was happening. My life had been happy and unmarred by tragedy. I was a devoted daughter and sister, had lots of friends, had gone to college, married a wonderful man, had two beautiful children, a home, hobbies—a blessed life. But breast cancer does not discriminate.

The surgery to remove my breast was uneventful, and breast reconstruction was not recommended for me at that time. Satisfied with my progress after a few days, the doctor was about to send me home. Needing the security of the hospital, I remember taking off my hospital gown in the shower and looking at myself for the first time. For some odd reason, I didn't cry, and I accepted what I saw. I had lost a breast, but I was alive and going to survive! I went home that day to begin my life again.

I began chemotherapy and had a rough time of it, needing a six-month leave of absence from work. I spent my days reading, writing in a journal, and visiting with family and friends. Between treatments, my husband took me on short vacations and to the movies. By the time Christmas rolled around, my treatments had ended, and I happily attended my husband's annual holiday party.

One day after showering, it became suddenly and painfully apparent that my right breast was gone. I was devastated! Then I realized that for many months, I had focused exclusively on the loss of my hair, not the loss of my breast. Now all I could see was a horizontal scar running across the right side of my chest. I was alone in my house, and tears flowed freely as I grieved for the loss.

My eighteen-year-old daughter asked if we could go shopping on Balboa Island, a cute little town nearby. We ferried over to the island to spend the day. As we entered the first shop, we noticed a display of paper tattoos of flowers, hearts, fish and seashells. We thought they were cute, purchased some strips of them, and returned to our beach house after several hours. According to the directions, after a few seconds with some warm water, they would be easy to apply, and we decorated our ankles and shoulders. After all, it was summer and a fun thing to do while on vacation.

The next morning transformed my life! I got up early, made some coffee, and sat outside celebrating a new day and looking at the beautiful ocean. Soon I decided to put on a bathing suit for another great day at the beach. Suddenly, seeing a strip of the recently purchased tattoos lying on the counter in the bathroom, I was struck with an idea: why not cut off a tattoo and place it over my mastectomy scar? I followed the simple directions, and, within seconds, my chest was adorned with a peach-colored rose! It was so pretty and feminine. I felt excited beyond belief: I had added a new accessory to my wardrobe and focused on a beautiful flower, not the scar.

Every day, I wore a paper tattoo. I wore flowers in the fall and spring, hearts on Valentine's Day, seashells on vacations, and even an "I Love You" in November to celebrate my wedding anniversary. For eleven years, I had elected not to undergo breast reconstructive surgery. Even without my breast, I was content to live my life, healthy and happy. It amazed me how paper tattoos changed the way I coped with the loss of my breast.

I still remember driving to a follow-up appointment with my oncologist. Suddenly, I realized that several days before I had applied a new tattoo and, in anticipation of my check-up, had not removed it. What would the doctor think? The moment arrived as he opened the front of the gown.

He broke into a huge smile. "I would *never* put anything past you! And that's one of the healthiest coping mechanisms I've ever seen! May I share your idea with other breast-cancer patients?" Of course, I was delighted.

I feel blessed to share my journey that began in 1982. Three years ago, I underwent reconstructive surgery and now celebrate a new right breast. I have recently been discharged from my oncologist's care; he declared me free of breast cancer.

I celebrate every single day of my life. I pray for continued good health and have participated with my daughter in the Revlon Run/Walk for breast and ovarian cancers. The event is held annually in Los Angeles in order to raise money to obliterate this terrible disease. Crossing the finish line was emotional and exhilarating for both of us.

I don't have the need to wear my paper tattoos anymore, but I have never discarded the ones I never used. I keep them in a special little box in a cabinet, and when I stumble across them, I see hearts and flowers and smile!

Joan Persky

Light

God allows us to experience the low points of life in order to teach us lessons we could learn in no other way.

                                                        C. S. Lewis

Cancer was not the first time I went to war with myself. Every fitting-room session was a battle, as was every crampy menstrual period, every saggy-eyed morning reflected in the mirror. From the time I was sixteen, I, like most women I knew, was in conflict with my body. I apologized for it often—jokingly at auditions, earnestly at photo sessions, shyly as I gave it for the first time to a geeky, sweetly bookish boy on the top bunk in his post-Salinger dorm room. As if a flat chest and broad thighs weren't bad enough, childbirth and time added thick ankles and stretch marks to the indictment. And I never did like my nose and my hair, and . . . well, let's not even go there.

But I never used the word "gargoyle" until I stared into the mirror at my blotchy post-surgery complexion, bloating above the gruesome biopsy scar secured by a four-inch chain of black stitches.

"My bride!" Gary teased, stalking me with his arms outstretched stiffly like Mary Shelley's monster. "Gloria
Frankensteinem."

I faced my fate with unwavering courage and a relatively small amount of cowardice and . . . oh, all right—
with drugs! Good drugs! The expensive kind! And lots of
'em! Praise God and pass the Valium.

Maybe that accounted for my Waldenesque post-biopsy
introspection. Whatever the catalyst, it did seem that in
the days following the diagnosis, the usual every day
noise had calmed considerably. Momentum that had
always carried me forward like a freight train rolled to a
halt. What had seemed the most pressing obligations were
now the least significant, and I couldn't help but see the
parallel between my denial of the long overdue changes
needed in my life and my denial of the cancer that had
already seeped from one small lymph node to both sides
of my neck and down toward my chest.

I'd always given away my time and efforts as easily as
an old lady offers knickknacks at a yard sale, asking little
and accepting even less. From Bunk Boy to bosses to the
PTA volunteer coordinator, no one ever had to beg for
their piece of me, and not recognizing that all those little
pieces added up to my life, I performed in overdrive to
make sure I surpassed their expectations. Now, for the
first time, my life was at the top of my agenda.

Women of my generation often don't know what to do
with that. We've grown accustomed to the concept that we
should be doing the work of at least two people, and we've
learned to pacify ourselves while our sleeping spirits slum-
ber on. But sooner or later the alarm goes off. We're forced
to open our eyes. And much to our surprise, there is light.

Joni Rodgers

"I've learned to stop worrying about
my body image, and love my reflection.
There you are . . . you fetching creature!"

I Can't Believe You

*There is only one history of any importance,
and it is the history of what you once believed in,
and the history of what you came to believe in.*

Kay Boyle

"I can't believe you tell people your age," my friend commented.

"Hey, I don't mind. Really! In fact, I love my age, because every single birthday means more than just presents and chocolate cake."

The day I heard the word "cancer" spoken by my doctor, life turned upside down.

"I have a test on Monday," I said foolishly, thinking he'd postpone surgery so I could ace my humanities test. I didn't realize I was preparing for the biggest test of my life.

Within hours, I discovered that I did have cancer. I learned at age thirty-two to face mortality—cancer had spread to my lymph nodes. Every time the doctors entered my room, they walked in with bad news and one more specialist. One white coat meant cancer. Two white coats meant chemo. Three meant radiation. Four meant detection of another possible tumor.

At one point, five doctors stood around my bed. It seemed fitting because the statistics had dropped to a 10 percent chance of surviving five years—one doctor for each year I might live.

There was a multitude of reasons to stick around—a husband of twelve years whom I loved a whole lot and three beautiful children who were clueless to the plight of their mom and dad, but who gave me daily strength in their innocent love and handmade gifts that hung on the hospital wall. To this day, I still have a crayon picture of me resting in bed, with a large head and larger lips and a thermometer sticking out of my mouth. The words "get well so u can com home" were my mantra.

I'm thankful for cancer in many ways. Does that sound crazy? I wouldn't wish it on anyone and don't want to go through it again, but it was a teacher. It helped me treasure every single day. It forced me to prioritize my life— things that were once important seemed foolish. It pushed me off the hamster wheel this society calls sacred and let me pursue the desires of my heart, instead of my wallet. It gave me the ability to see life as fragile, not one day promised. It allowed me to treasure my three beautiful children, who sometimes brought heartache along with joy as they grew up, who are all now in college and can now spell beautifully.

When I hit my fifth year of survival, I left my job to write full-time. I decided not to write one more word about anything that didn't matter to me. It was a step of faith, but made perfect sense. Cancer taught me not to let the opportunities of your heart pass you by because none of us are promised "one day" or "someday."

On my fortieth birthday, I rode go-carts with thirty of my closest friends to celebrate. The numbers 4-0 hanging across the wall were a beautiful sight. I celebrated my tenth year of survival on a boat in the Amazon in the rain-forest of Brazil. I sat on the top level and watched the sun rise, and from somewhere deep inside, I thanked God for the opportunity to experience life through facing death.

You see, life has become a series of celebrations. Last month, I celebrated my thirteenth year of survival and embraced my forty-fourth birthday. Next month, Richard and I will celebrate our twenty-fourth anniversary. Leslie, our oldest, turned twenty-one last year, and our twins are twenty . . . young adults now—all running after their own dreams, which my bout with cancer taught them, too.

I look at my friend and answer her question. Do I mind telling my age? Absolutely not! I'll shout it from the rooftops: I'm forty-four! I'm thankful for all ten gray hairs (though I will cover them with honey ash brown and romantic red highlights). When I look in the mirror and notice the small lines appearing around my mouth and eyes, I don't call them wrinkles. I call them opportunities. Every line was placed there by a smile that creased my face—an experience, large or small, that came from living this gift called life.

T. Suzanne Eller

The Big "C"

"The Big 'C'" I heard someone call it.
Another just whispered the word.
That we don't even dare to say "cancer" out loud
Gives it power it doesn't deserve.

So I'm giving that letter new meaning
And refusing to give in to fear
By reclaiming the power for you and for me
And by saying these words loud and clear:

Let the "C" be for "Cure" and "Compassion."
Let it stand for the "Candles" we light.
And a "Chorus" of voices shouting "You Can!"
To all who will take up this fight.

Let the "C" be for "Cash Contribution"
("Credit" or "Check" will work, too).
Let it stand for "Commitment" and "Checkups"
And "Cheer,"
And the "Children" "Counting" on you.

Let it mean that we know our "Creator"
Is beside us each step of the way,
And remind us to "Call" on his strength and his love
And to "Celebrate" every new day.

To everyone facing this "Challenge,"
I say it's a fight we can win.
Tell all who will listen, that starting today,
The "C" is for "Courage" my friend.

Kathy Cawthon

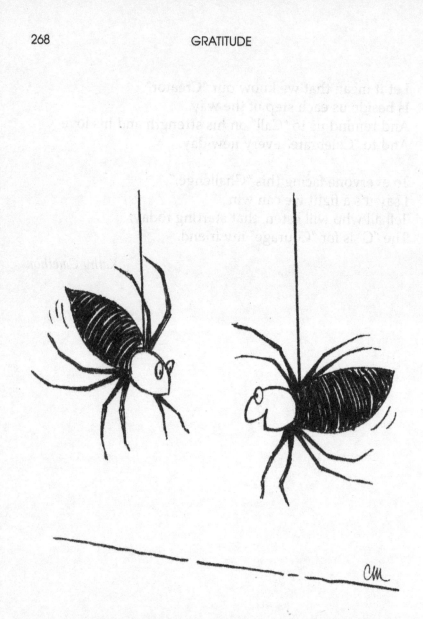

"I feel a lot better now since I found so much information about cancer treatments on the web."

Who Is Jack Canfield?

Jack Canfield is the co-creator and editor of the *Chicken Soup for the Soul®* series, which *Time* magazine has called "the publishing phenomenon of the decade." The series now has 105 titles with over 100 million copies in print in forty-one languages. Jack is also the co-author of eight other bestselling books including *The Success Principles™: How to Get from Where You Are to Where You Want to Be, Dare to Win, The Aladdin Factor, You've Got to Read This Book, The Power of Focus: How to Hit Your Business, Personal and Financial Targets with Absolute Certainty.*

Jack has recently developed a telephone coaching program and an online coaching program based on his most recent book *The Success Principles.* He also offers a seven-day Breakthrough to Success seminar every summer, which attracts 400 people from fifteen countries around the world.

Jack is the CEO of Chicken Soup for the Soul Enterprises and the Canfield Training Group in Santa Barbara, California, and Founder of the Foundation for Self-Esteem in Culver City, California. He has conducted intensive personal and professional development seminars on the principles of success for over 900,000 people in twenty-one countries around the world. He has spoken to hundreds of thousands of others at numerous conferences and conventions and has been seen by millions of viewers on national television shows such as *The Today Show, Fox and Friends, Inside Edition, Hard Copy, CNN's Talk Back Live, 20/20, Eye to Eye,* and the *NBC Nightly News* and the *CBS Evening News.*

Jack is the recipient of many awards and honors, including three honorary doctorates and a Guinness World Records Certificate for having seven *Chicken Soup for the Soul* books appearing on the *New York Times* bestseller list on May 24, 1998.

To write to Jack or for inquiries about Jack as a speaker, his coaching programs or his seminars, use the following contact information:

Jack Canfield
The Canfield Companies
P.O. Box 30880
Santa Barbara, CA 93130
Phone: 805-563-2935; Fax: 805-563-2945
E-mail: *info@jackcanfield.com*
Web site: *www.jackcanfield.com*

Who Is Mark Victor Hansen?

In the area of human potential, no one is more respected than Mark Victor Hansen. For more than thirty years, Mark has focused solely on helping people from all walks of life reshape their personal vision of what's possible. His powerful messages of possibility, opportunity and action have created powerful change in thousands of organizations and millions of individuals worldwide.

He is a sought-after keynote speaker, bestselling author and marketing maven. Mark's credentials include a lifetime of entrepreneurial success and an extensive academic background. He is a prolific writer with many bestselling books, such as *The One Minute Millionaire, The Power of Focus, The Aladdin Factor* and *Dare to Win,* in addition to the *Chicken Soup for the Soul* series. Mark has made a profound influence through his library of audios, videos and articles in the areas of big thinking, sales achievement, wealth building, publishing success, and personal and professional development.

Mark is the founder of the MEGA Seminar Series. MEGA Book Marketing University and Building Your MEGA Speaking Empire are annual conferences where Mark coaches and teaches new and aspiring authors, speakers and experts on building lucrative publishing and speaking careers. Other MEGA events include MEGA Marketing Magic and My MEGA Life.

He has appeared on *Oprah, CNN* and *The Today Show,* he has been quoted in *Time, U.S. News & World Report, USA Today, New York Times* and *Entrepreneur* and had countless radio interviews, assuring our planet's people that "You can easily create the life you deserve."

As a philanthropist and humanitarian, Mark works tirelessly for organizations such as Habitat for Humanity, American Red Cross, March of Dimes, Childhelp USA and many others. He is the recipient of numerous awards that honor his entrepreneurial spirit, philanthropic heart and business acumen. He is a lifetime member of the Horatio Alger Association of Distinguished Americans, an organization that honored Mark with the prestigious Horatio Alger Award for his extraordinary life achievements.

Mark Victor Hansen is an enthusiastic crusader of what's possible and is driven to make the world a better place.

Mark Victor Hansen & Associates, Inc.
P.O. Box 7665
Newport Beach, CA 92658
phone: 949-764-2640
fax: 949-722-6912
Web site: *www.markvictorhansen.com*

Who Is Mary Olsen Kelly?

Mary Olsen Kelly is an author, business owner, public speaker and breast-cancer survivor. Her books include *Path of the Pearl: Discover Your Treasures Within* (Beyond Words Publishing), *The #1 Best Tools and Tips from the Trenches of Breast Cancer* (Books Beyond Borders), *Finding Each Other* and *Treasury of Light: An Anthology of the Best in New Age Literature* (both published by Simon and Schuster).

Books Beyond Borders has recently contracted with Mary to write three more *Tips from the Trenches* books: *Chemotherapy, Eating to Beat Cancer* and *Complementary and Alternative Healing Techniques for Cancer.*

She is an advocate for breast-cancer funding and research, and is the director of Breast Wishes Institute, an educational nonprofit foundation that hosts the Web site BreastWishes.org. The organization distributes educational information about breast cancer and is dedicated to educating, inspiring and supporting people with breast cancer. Breast Wishes Puppetry Company is currently researching, writing and producing "My Mommy's Bald," a puppet production that will be made into a film.

Mary is a dynamic and entertaining speaker who enthralls audiences with her lectures on healing. She loves speaking to breast-cancer organizations, medical organizations and women's groups of all kinds. She has been a featured lecturer on Holland America and Princess Cruise Ships.

With her husband, Don Kelly, she owns the Black Pearl Gallery fine jewelry stores in Maui and Honolulu, Hawaii, and Balboa Island, California.

To schedule Mary for a speech, contact:

Chicken Soup for the Breast Cancer Survivor's Soul
575 Cooke St., Suite A, Box 3013
Honolulu, HI 96813
E-mail: CS4BCSoul@aol.com

Web sites: *BreastWishes.org* and *PathofthePearl.com*

Contributors

Donna Andres lives in Branford, Connecticut, with her husband and children.

Pam Arciero is a puppeteer, director and actress for television, stage and film. Her credits include *Sesame Street, Between the Lions,* and numerous commercials, films and off-Broadway shows. She holds degrees from the University of Hawaii and the University of Connecticut.

Jami Bernard is a film critic for the *New York Daily News* and a breast cancer survivor. She is the author of seven books, including *Breast Cancer: There & Back* (Warner Books, 2001).

Jennifer Basye Sander is a *New York Times* bestselling author and an Emmy-award winning television producer. A popular public speaker, she lives in Granite Bay, California, with her husband, writer Peter Sander, and their sons Julian and Jonathan. You can reach her at *basyesander@yahoo.com.*

Denise Blunk is the manager of the Susan G. Komen Breast Cancer Foundation Grand Rapids Affiliate. She is active in local support groups such as Gilda's Club and a Breast Health Coalition. Denise resides in Caledonia, Michigan, with her husband, Jim, and daughter, Adrianna. She enjoys reading, volleyball and shopping! Please reach her at *grkomen@unitedwaycares.com.*

Sharon Bomgaars is a wife, mother, nana and former reading teacher. Her hobbies include traveling with her husband of thirty-nine years, spending time with her family, teaching an ESL class and working in her church. Her dream is to someday write a children's book for her beautiful grandchildren.

Arlette Braman is a freelance writer with many articles to her credit and the author of six nonfiction children's books. When not writing, she indulges in her passion—sailing on the Chesapeake Bay. Arlette lives in Maryland and enjoys quality time with her two teenagers, family and friends. She is a four-time breast-cancer survivor. Arlette may be contacted via e-mail at *arlnb@mac.com* or on her Web site at *www.arlettebraman.com.*

Mary Anne Breen—Former Miss Colorado USA, model, cruise line DSM, mortgage L/O—finally found her Legacy as an Independent Business Owner with her husband, John, and son, Connor. She credits God's grace, her Christian community, family, friends, business mentors—all who helped her breeze through eight chemo and thrity three radiation treatments. If she thought her breast would one day get her published, she wasn't thinking cancer or book! She now cherishes all her titles: Christian, Wife, Mother, Survivor. Contact her at *heart2hand@convad.net.*

Anthony Burton received his bachelor of arts in exercise and sports science from the UNC-Chapel Hill in 1998. He resides in Charlotte, North Carolina, where he works as a project manager and a personal trainer. He aspires to be an author of children's books. Please e-mail him at *anthonyb235@yahoo.com.*

Ellen Ann Callahan received her law degree from the University of Baltimore in 1977. She practices adoption law. Ellen enjoys being married, raising her two children, gardening, writing, playing poker and traveling on cruise ships. She also dances whenever she hears a beat. Please e-mail her at *callahanea@comcast.net.*

Leah Cano holds a master's degree in education and has worked as an elementary-school teacher. She has written for *MAMM Magazine, The Desert Woman Magazine* and *Transitions Abroad Magazine.* She has a deep love of travel and languages. She resides in Laguna Beach, California, where she continues to pursue a writing career.

Sue Caruso has lived in the Pacific Northwest for the past thirty-seven years. In addition to being a swimmer, she is an artist, voracious reader and community volunteer. Her sense of humor has no boundaries. Please e-mail her at *sbcaruso42@yahoo.com.*

Kathy Cawthon and her husband, Roger, were diagnosed with cancer at the same time. They are now ten-year survivors! Kathy graduated from the College of William & Mary, and she is the author of *Medicine, Marathons and Miracles: Turning a Diagnosis of Cancer into Personal Victory.* Please e-mail her at *kcawthon@cox.net.*

Kathy Chamberlin received her bachelor of science with honors in 1980. Her poetry has been published internationally. She has successfully fought breast cancer three times and can be reached at P.O. Box 1052, LaGrange Park, IL 60526.

A native of Norfolk, Virginia, **Ida Chipman**, a prize-winning journalist, is the wife of attorney and retired Appellate and Marshall County Judge Eugene Chipman. She has been a correspondent for the *South Bend Tribune* for the past eleven years and has had stories published in twenty-seven newspapers and several magazines and trade journals.

Donna St. Jean Conti is a breast-cancer survivor and cocreator of Next Level Survivor, an exercise program designed to address the special needs of post-surgery breast-cancer patients. She is a marketing communications professional and owner of St. Conti Communications in Mission Viejo, California. Contact her at *stconti@cox.net.*

Barbara Curtis obtained a bachelor of arts from Evergreen State College in Olympia, Washington, in 1977. She's owned three businesses, two with her sister (custom clothing shops in Walnut Creek, California, and Lahaina, Maui) and an international book sales and consulting venture called Books Beyond Borders/Curtis Int'l. She enjoys cooking, traveling, most outdoor activities, and the company of her good friends and wonderful family. She's very happily married to Chuck Curtis, with her twenty-year wedding anniversary approaching.

Susan Darke is the director of human resources for an IT company in Virginia. She is a volunteer with the Y-ME Breast Cancer Support Group, serving as a match for newly diagnosed women. She enjoys reading, dancing, singing, sunny days and long walks on the beach.

John de Strakosch is an author who lives in southern California with his wife and their two dogs. His book, *Healing Sword: Creating and Maintaining an Exquisite Life*, is an inspiration to many and is available from the author. Please e-mail him at *mindbody@mindspring.com*.

Teri Reath D'Ignazio is a career travel agent (thirty years). During her breast cancer treatment, she took a work sabbatical and became very involved in her community, particularly environmental issues. Teri is married and has one daughter, Curry. She enjoys quilting, traveling and ran for local office in November 2005. Please contact her at *teri_myworld@yahoo.com*.

Regina Dodson is a teaching assistant at a local school. She is thankful for her husband, Tom, and sons, Michael and Tom, for their love and support. She plans on retiring at her lake home where she can watch the sun dance on the water, giving her peace and hope.

Carol Ross Edmonston received her B.S. from the University of Southern California in 1970. She is now an international inspirational speaker and offers creative workshops on the Magic and Wisdom of Doodling. She is an ardent student of meditation and enjoys hiking, fishing and traveling. Please e-mail her at *Carol@SacredDoodles.com*.

T. Suzanne Eller is an author and freelance speaker from Oklahoma. She has been featured on numerous national media programs, including *Focus on the Family* and *Aspiring Women*. She ministers to teens and families and can be reached at *http://realteenfaith.com* or *tseller@daretobelieve.org*.

Sally Fouché lives in Bellevue, Washington, with her husband and three children. This story's subject, Chris Helmholz, continues to inspire all. Sally graduated from the University of Puget Sound, with honors in economics, and worked in the computer and banking industry. She can be reached at *sallyfouche@yahoo.com*.

Lowell Gere is a nine-year breast-cancer survivor. He is retired and lives in the northwest with his wife Betty. They enjoy travel and their grandchildren. He enjoys playing golf and is an active volunteer in organizations related to cancer and breast cancer. He can be reached at *lagere@earthlink.net*.

Judy Hague is currently on disability for her cancer. She enjoys reading, scrapbooking and writing. Her real love is writing poetry, and she has been published twice. Judy is currently writing a small book about her experience with cancer and hopes to be able to share it with others. E-mail her at *judyhague@bellsouth.net*.

Heather Haldeman began writing professionally six years ago. She has been married to her husband, Hank, for twenty-six years and has three children. She has published several personal essays and is currently writing a book on growing up in Los Angeles. Please reach her at *Heathheh@aol.com*.

Susan R. Harris is a professor in the School of Rehabilitation Sciences at the University of British Columbia in Vancouver. A breast cancer researcher, Susan was one of the original members of Abreast in a Boat, the world's first Dragon Boat team comprised entirely of women living with breast cancer.

Jonny Hawkins loves creating cartoons. Over the last twenty years, his work has appeared in over 300 publications and in over 100 books. He has several books out including *Laughter From the Pearly Gates* and *The Awesome Book of Heavenly Humor*. He can be reached at *jonnyhawkins2nz.@yahoo.com*.

Judith Averitt Hayes is a three-time breast-cancer survivor. She started a support group for survivors in her hometown of Winchester, Kentucky, in 1995. Judith is very active in the American Cancer Society's Relay for Life and a participant in the Susan G. Komen Race for the Cure. She and her husband, Walter, have been married for forty-six years. They have two daughters and five wonderful grandchildren.

Jacqueline M. Hickey lives, runs and writes in Rockport, Massachusetts. You can contact her at *Roxie01966@yahoo.com*.

Allan Hirsh, M.A. is a psychotherapist, trainer and cartoonist. His latest book, *Relax For the Fun of It: A Cartoon & Audio Guide to Releasing Stress*, is available at *www.xaramal.com*. Contact Allan at *relax@allanhirsh.com* or 705-476-2219 (North Bay, Ontario). Web site *www.allanhirsh.com*.

Leigh Anne Jasheway is a freelance humor writer who won the Erma Bombeck Humor Writing competition with this article. She believes in a previous lifetime she may have left the iron on. E-mail her at *www.accidentalcomic.com*.

Don Kelly is the owner of the Black Pearl Gallery stores on Maui, Oahu, and Balboa Island, California. He loves to travel the world finding inspiration for his unique and exotic jewelry designs.

Ruth Kotler received her BS in Biology from Stonehill College and her Physician Associate Degree from Yale School of Medicine. She is a Physician Associate at the University of Connecticut Health Center. She resides in Avon, Connecticut with her husband, David, and children Nathan and Hannah.

Pandora Kurth lives in Maui, Hawaii. Pandora has been a licensed massage therapist for sixteen years. She has been writing since her early years. Her first published story was in 1969. Her passions include working in the Healing Arts, writing, collecting vintage Hawaiiana and living "Aloha."

Mary Ellen "Barney" LaFavers is a retired nurse who lives in Somerset, Kentucky. She was diagnosed with breast cancer over thirty years ago. Mary Ellen is a mother, grandmother, great-grandmother and great-great-grandmother. Her nickname, "Barney," was an affectionate derivation from her maiden name during nurse's training and has stuck ever since.

Ryan Matthew Landis is an elementary-school teacher in Lancaster, Pennsylvania. He's written two books, including *The Pink Ribbon Boys*, a children's book about two brothers whose football season takes a turn after their mother is diagnosed with breast cancer. More information and his e-mail address can be found at *www.pinkribbonboys.com*.

Ron Lando-Brown and his wife Micki live on the island of Maui. Their vacation rental business brings them people and stories from all over the world.

Betsy Ludwig is originally from San Francisco, California. She has a son and family in San Jose and a daughter and family in San Mateo. She moved to

Honolulu, Hawaii, twenty-five years ago. Betsy loved teaching in California and Hawaii and is now in her tenth year of retirement. Her volunteer work fills a great space in her life. You can e-mail Betsy at *betsylu30@aol.com.*

Charles Markman has been in the art business since high school. He operated a graphic desing studio in the Chicago area and freelanced as a cartoonist for many years. Stil drawing cartoons and very involved in watercolors painting and pen and ink drawings, Charles can be reached by e-mail at *cngmarkman@aol.com.*

Doug Manuel is a mathematician who writes poetry as a balance to stressful situations. His wife, Josie, is a breast-cancer survivor of four years. They have two daughters and two grandchildren and enjoy them all very much. He lives on five acres in Gig Harbor, Washington, with two cats, a dog and a goose.

Tina Wagner Mattern, a Portland, Oregon, writer, is a healthy five-year survivor. Foregoing conventional treatments, she put her faith in God. He prescribed love, good nutrition, natural hormones and humor. This story is excerpted from her upcoming book, *When Good Boobs Go Bad. . . .* E-mail her at *tinamattern@earthlink.net.*

Lorna Maxwell is a native southern Californian. She has been an elementary-school teacher for seventeen years. Lorna likes to spend time with her wonderful husband, precocious daughter, two funny cats and their very energetic Jack Russell terriers. She also enjoys singing, playing piano and directing the children's choir at church.

Maria McNaught attended Northeastern University. She is married and has two children. She enjoys writing and has published a children's book called *Grandma's Ashanti Cloth.* Please contact her at *marmcn@mariamcnaught.com.*

For twenty-one years, **Dr. Suzanne Metzger** has been captivating audiences with her keynote addresses. Her goal is to help people understand the incredible power of soft skills. She is the author of *Learning Through Living . . . Some Assembly Required* and coauthor of *The Complete Idiot's Guide to Living with Breast Cancer.* Please e-mail her at *suzannecmi@earthlink.net* or visit *www.corporatemasters.com.*

Lori Misicka is a professional speaker who helps people bounce back from all kinds of adversity. Her down-to-earth techniques were developed during twenty years of managing customers and staff in the broadcast industry and put to the test when she was diagnosed with breast cancer. Contact Lori at *lori@howtofeelgoodwhenyoufeelbad.com.*

Sherrie Page Najarian received her bachelor of science in nursing with honors at the University of North Carolina at Chapel Hill. She received her master of science in nursing from Yale University. Sherrie enjoys writing personal essays and is currently working on a young-adult novel.

Jennie Nash is the author of *The Victoria's Secret Catalog Never Stops Coming and Other Lessons I Learned from Breast Cancer* (Scribner, 2001). A five-year breast-cancer survivor at the age of forty-one, she is a popular speaker at breast-cancer survival celebrations across the country.

Joan Persky received her bachelor of arts degree in English literature in 1967.

She is a substitute teacher in Calabasas, California, and especially enjoys helping children with their writing assignments. She has been a volunteer in the Los Angeles Unified School District for the Reading by Nines program. Joan enjoys reading novels and short stories, traveling worldwide, and playing the piano. Please e-mail her at *playz88@aol.com.*

Pamela Pierce has been married to her high-school sweetheart for thirty-four years. She has two wonderful children and three beautiful grandchildren. She enjoys reading, sewing and interior decorating. You can e-mail her at *grandmapam@woh.rr.com.*

Stephaine Piro lives in New Hampshire with her husband, daughter and three cats. She is one of King Features' team of women cartoonists, "Six Chix" (she is the Saturday chick!). Her single panel "Fair Game" apears in newspapers and on her Web site *www.stephaniepiro.com.* She also designs gift items for her company Strip T's. Contact her at *piro@worldpath.net.*

Michele V. Price is the director of study abroad and international exchanges at Western Oregon University. She has lived and worked in Oregon since 1979. She is an eighteen-year breast-cancer survivor who learned during her healing process that literature, writing and the creative imagination can transform people and teach them to live well and to die well. She was a winner in the Oregon State Poetry Association's Fall 2001 contest, and her poems have appeared in *Manzanita Quarterly* and *Verseweavers.*

Rhonda Richards-Cohen, a graduate of Greenville College and Stanford University, resides in Dallas with her stepchildren and husband Todd. His motto—"no more somedays"—changed the way they live with metastatic disease. An eight-year survivor, Rhonda retired from producing instructional multimedia to write her memoirs, pursue health and practice parenting.

Lee Scheinman attended Oglethorpe University in Atlanta. Her career involved many phases of the music business and later advertising. She currently lives in St. Simons Island, Georgia. There she continues cancer fundraising. Lee is an active Rotarian and volunteers teaching math to high-school dropouts.

Bonnie Seibert was raised in Merrillville, Indiana. She went to Hammond Junior College and studied IBM Keypunch. Bonnie is married to Harry Seibert and is a housewife. They have one son, a daughter-in-law and three grandchildren. Bonnie enjoys reading, sewing and quilting.

Pamela Shandel is an imagist and adventuress. She writes and photographs stories, and she plays tournament poker internationally. She has a master's of professional writing from USC. She was the first of three females to graduate Ringling Bros. Barnum & Bailey Circus Clown College, opening the way for women to become clowns in America. Pamela is finishing her first novel about thriving even if one is not a "normal" kind of person. Pamela loves laughing and celebrations.

Kathryn O. Sharr trained at Hartford Secretarial School in the late 1930s and greatly enjoyed her career as an executive secretary. After raising her two children, she traveled extensively with her husband in the U.S., Europe, and

Central and South America. Kathryn has two grandchildren and many nieces and nephews who consider her their "second mom." She credits her family, friends and faith as sustaining forces in her life.

Lillie Shockney is author of *Breast Cancer Survivors' Club: A Nurse's Experience* and *Journey of Hope*. She is director of the Johns Hopkins Breast Center. She is a national speaker on this disease and an oncology nurse. E-mail her at *shockli@jhmi.edu*.

Myra Shostak is a writer and teacher with master's degrees in child development and social work. She is the author of *Rainbow Candles: A Chanukah Counting Book*. Myra enjoys calligraphy, bookbinding, writing, quilting, working with children and learning new things. She can be reached at *MyraC345@msn.com*.

Nanci L. Stroupe has been writing for many years and has had numerous stories printed on various Web sites. Three of her stories have been published in *Heartwarmers of Love, Half Full* and *Stories for a Woman's Heart*. She enjoys reading and spending time with her husband, Douglas, of forty-six years, the love of her life. She also enjoys her two daughters, son-in-law and six wonderful grandchildren. She would love to write an inspirational book of her life to give hope when there seems to be none.

An actress, **Lolly Susi** has worked in London's West End, on BBC-TV/Radio, and in such films as *Dirty Rotten Scoundrels, Proof* and *The Jacket*. Lolly's first play was produced by the Hampstead Theatre, and her book about the Central School of Speech and Drama will be published in 2006.

Karen Theis is a hairstylist, wife, mother and two-time cancer survivor. She says, "My stories are my own cancer experiences. I write from my heart. My mission is to reach out and encourage ladies with cancer." Karen has been awarded the Valley True Award and the Community Builders Award. She speaks to various groups about living a positive life.

Kathy Vancura was raised in Hamtramck, Michigan, along with six brothers and sisters. She currently resides in Orange County, California, with husband Tony and children Christopher (11) and Emily (8). Kathy was diagnosed with breast cancer in 1998 within weeks of her older sister, MaryAnn. Both are now eight-year survivors. E-mail Kathy at *tonkathvan@sbcglobal.net*.

Diana von Welenetz Wentworth, a popular public speaker and television host, is the author of many award-winning books and coauthor of *Chicken Soup for the Soul Cookbook* and *Chicken Soup to Inspire the Body and Soul*. Her romantic memoir, *Send Me Someone,* is soon to be a feature film.

Beverly Vote is a Certified Healing Images specialist. She facilitates workshops that teach how to empower mind, body and spirit for a deeper healing experience. She is completing a program for breast cancer to help women reclaim their healing and feminine spirit. Contact her at *beverlyvote@aol.com* or *www.breastcancerwellness.org*.

Paula Young received her bachelor of arts from Lone Mountain College and later earned her California teaching credential. She is the mother of two grown daughters and grandmother of four. Currently retired, she enjoys volunteering in her community, her walking group, needlework and traveling. Please e-mail her at *pawyo@snowcrest.net*.

Elaine Zalar works in the medical field. Breast cancer has struck six members of her family. She speaks openly about the experience and continues to be an inspiration to her family and friends. She has a son and enjoys traveling with her husband on their Harley. E-mail her at *mzalar@alltel.net*.

Permissions

We would like to acknowledge the many publishers and individuals who granted us permission to reprint the cited material. (Note: The stories that were written by Jack Canfield, Mark Victor Hansen, or Mary Olsen Kelly are not included in this listing.)

She's My Hero. Reprinted by permission of Anthony Burton. ©2004 Anthony Burton.

Night School. Reprinted by permission of Kathy Cawthon. ©2000 Kathy Cawthon.

Sooner or Later. Reprinted by permission of Lori Misicka. ©2002 Lori Misicka.

Family. Reprinted by permission of Lowell Gere. ©2003 Lowell Gere.

You'll Never Feel So Loved. Reprinted by permission of Sharon Bomgaars. ©2004 Sharon Bomgaars.

Food Is Love. Reprinted by permission of Barbara Curtis. ©2005 Barbara Curtis.

All You Need Is Love. Reprinted by permission of Christina Maria Mattern. ©2003 Christina Maria Mattern.

Reading Charlotte's Web. Reprinted by permission of Jennie Nash. ©2005 Jennie Nash.

Locks of Love. Reprinted by permission of Leah Cano and Mamm Magazine. ©2002 Leah Cano and Mamm Magazine.

He Doesn't Take "No" for an Answer. Reprinted by permission of Maurice J. Leavitt. ©2002 Maurice J. Leavitt.

Giving and Receiving. Reprinted by permission of Jennie Nash. ©2001 Jennie Nash.

Little Man Christopher. Reprinted by permission of Kathy Vancura. ©2003 Kathy Vancura.

Debbie's Story. Reprinted by permission of Yvonne Lolly Susi. ©2003 Yvonne Lolly Susi.

Enjoy Life! Reprinted by permission of Regina Dodson. ©2003 Regina Dodson.

Filler. Reprinted by permission of Bonnie Seibert. ©2003 Bonnie Seibert.

Heart Massage. Reprinted by permission of Pandora Kurth. ©2001 Pandora Kurth.

My Heroes. Reprinted by permission of Maria McNaught. ©2002 Maria McNaught.

"Tweety Conquers That Mean Old Bweast Cancer." Reprinted by permission of Susan Darke. ©2003 Susan Darke.

Blessed by Friends. Reprinted by permission of Judy Hague. ©2003 Judy Hague.

The Glow Girls. Reprinted by permission of Karen Theis. ©1999 Karen Theis.

Bring on the Lasagna! Reprinted by permission of Lorna Maxwell. ©2003 Lorna Maxwell.

The Seasons of Our Lives. Reprinted by permission of Diana von Welenetz Wentworth. ©2004 Diana von Welenetz Wentworth.

You've Got to Play If You Want to Win. Reprinted by permission of Lori Elise Misicka. ©2002 Lori Elise Misicka.

A "Gift of Healing" Journey. Reprinted by permission of Betsy Ludwig. ©2005 Betsy Ludwig.

Isabelle and Her Dollies' Hair. Reprinted by permission of Paula Young. ©2005 Paula Young.

The Bus Ride. Reprinted by permission of John de Strakosch. ©2003 John de Strakosch. *He Does Not Live in Vain.* Reprinted by permission of Dr. Suzanne Metzger. ©2003 Dr. Suzanne Metzger.

Stop Changing! Reprinted by permission of Rhonda Richards-Cohen. ©2005 Rhonda Richards-Cohen.

"Shoot the Messengers." Reprinted by permission of Don Kelly. ©2003 Don Kelly.

Angel Hugh. Reprinted by permission of Yvonne Lolly Susi. ©2003 Yvonne Lolly Susi.

Knowing What Your Rope Is. Reprinted by permission of Myra Shostak. ©1988 Myra Shostak.

A Message from My Marine. Reprinted by permission of Kathy Cawthon. ©2002 Kathy Cawthon.

My Red Badges of Courage. Reprinted by permission of Donna St. Jean Conti. ©2004 Donna St. Jean Conti.

Courage Comes in All Colors. Reprinted by permission of Jennie Nash. ©2001 Jennie Nash.

Courage to Climb. Reprinted by permission of Michele V. Price. ©2002 Michele V. Price.

Abreast in a Dragon Boat. Reprinted by permission of Susan Harris and Mamm Magazine. ©2000 Susan Harris and Mamm Magazine.

Racing for the Cure. Reprinted by permission of Ellen Ann Callahan. ©2003 Ellen Ann Callahan.

For Josie. Reprinted by permission of Doug Manuel. ©2001 Doug Manuel.

Fifty-One-Year Survivor!. Reprinted by permission of Kathryn O. Sharr. ©2003 Kathryn O. Sharr.

All the Gifts. Reprinted by permission of Pam Arciero. ©2003 Pam Arciero.

Dancing at Evan's Wedding. Reprinted by permission of Nancy Jaynes and Ida Chipman. ©2000 Nancy Jaynes and Ida Chipman.

Joy Is the Simplest Form of Gratitude. Reprinted by permission of Karen Theis. ©2005 Karen Theis.

A Time to Listen. Reprinted by permission of Donna Andres. ©2003 Donna Andres.

Improving Your Life Every Day

Real people sharing real stories—for nineteen years. Now, Chicken Soup for the Soul has gone beyond the bookstore to become a world leader in life improvement. Through books, movies, DVDs, online resources and other partnerships, we bring hope, courage, inspiration and love to hundreds of millions of people around the world. Chicken Soup for the Soul's writers and readers belong to a one-of-a-kind global community, sharing advice, support, guidance, comfort, and knowledge.

Chicken Soup for the Soul stories have been translated into more than 40 languages and can be found in more than one hundred countries. Every day, millions of people experience a Chicken Soup for the Soul story in a book, magazine, newspaper or online. As we share our life experiences through these stories, we offer hope, comfort and inspiration to one another. The stories travel from person to person, and from country to country, helping to improve lives everywhere.

Chicken Soup for the Soul®

Share with Us

We all have had Chicken Soup for the Soul moments in our lives. If you would like to share your story or poem with millions of people around the world, go to chickensoup.com and click on "Submit Your Story." You may be able to help another reader, and become a published author at the same time. Some of our past contributors have launched writing and speaking careers from the publication of their stories in our books!

Our submission volume has been increasing steadily — the quality and quantity of your submissions has been fabulous. We only accept story submissions via our website. They are no longer accepted via mail or fax.

To contact us regarding other matters, please send us an e-mail through webmaster@chickensoupforthesoul.com, or fax or write us at:

Chicken Soup for the Soul
P.O. Box 700
Cos Cob, CT 06807-0700
Fax: 203-861-7194

One more note from your friends at Chicken Soup for the Soul: Occasionally, we receive an unsolicited book manuscript from one of our readers, and we would like to respectfully inform you that we do not accept unsolicited manuscripts and we must discard the ones that appear.

An excerpt from:

Chicken Soup for the Soul.

The Cancer Book

101 Stories of Courage, Support & Love

Jack Canfield,
Mark Victor Hansen & David Tabatsky

Includes the inspirational memoir, *It's Just a Word*,
by Elizabeth Bayer

It's Not the Answer.
It's the Question.

A s the doctor pointed at the blue, shape-shifting blobs moving across a darkened screen, I tried to be analytical even as I was feeling devastated. I tried to appear hopeful, while all I heard was one word: malignant. Ever since my doctor had said the c-word along with my name, both in the same sentence, all I really saw was my life slipping away, vanishing before my eyes.

My thoughts raced in a hundred directions. I'm only forty-four, too young to leave behind the people who love me. And my five Labradors, my Jack Russell—what about them? Would they feel as if I'd abandoned them? Wonder what they'd done wrong?

For the past year, I'd been dealing with my mother's battle against her own inoperable cancer. Then, a week before my surgery, my father was rushed to the hospital for an emergency procedure, a complication from his colon cancer.

I'd blinked, and suddenly we were all struggling for our lives.

I wondered: Why me? A ridiculous question when you think about it, really, because there's no logical answer. Cancer is what happens to other people, people who don't take good care of themselves, people exposed to insidious carcinogens or deadly asbestos, people living under power lines. People just like me.

I heard voices. Not the kind that come from an unbalanced

mind—just the opposite, because these voices came with clarity, and that was the problem. The truth had never been an issue for me. I'm a curious person. I've often been criticized for trying to make sense of the senseless. But this cancer coming out of nowhere, I realized, would be my toughest test of all.

I tried to accept the challenge but didn't get far. If there was a lesson, I just wasn't learning it. If there was a blessing, I didn't feel it. There was no inspiration, no revelation. No matter how hard I tried to make things fit, I couldn't. At the end of the day, I still had cancer and no suitable explanation.

Was I going crazy? Had the stress from my diagnosis forced some sort of break with reality? It seemed possible. On the outside, my world was in turmoil. It would have been easy to fall apart, but instead, I did the opposite. I pulled everything together.

Facing my own mortality forced me to prioritize.

I heard something, nothing audible, but it was very clear and very powerful, and there was no mistaking the message: Cancer wasn't just about me; it actually involved everyone else. My world began shifting toward a more universal consciousness. In life, there are no bad experiences, only lessons. It's easy to get caught up in a crisis, but if you're only watching the ball, then you're missing the game. Shifting your focus beyond the obvious is the real game and I was somehow learning how to play.

How many times in the past had I looked at a problem and found the outcome to be more valuable than what caused it in the first place? A light bulb began to blink above my head. Isn't how I react to disorder ultimately what will free me from it?

The tougher questions lay beneath the surface: if I didn't survive this, would my life have been everything I'd wanted it to be? Would there be apologies left unsaid? Forgiveness denied? Had I done everything I could to leave the world a little better than it was before I got here?

On the flipside—and perhaps most important—if I survived this, would I make a daily commitment to those same principles?

They removed the cancer early enough and even saved my

kidney. That's the good news. The bad news—if you want to call it that—is that it may return. There are two spots on my other kidney. They, too, might be malignant. That my cancer is a rare, hereditary form increases the likelihood. The doctor says all we can do is watch and wait.

CT scans will likely become a way of life for me, something I'll have to live with for a long time, but I refuse to see them as constant reminders of the deadly intruder lurking within my cell structure. For me, they are reminders of something else, something much more important. They remind me of time, my most priceless commodity. It's not about how much of it I have. It's about how much I do with it.

Living each day like it's your last is like climbing the tallest mountain in the world. It doesn't matter how long you get to look down. Just being able to see it makes every second priceless and every step well worth the trip.

I didn't really know that before. The disease has changed that.

The way I to respond to cancer will reveal its true meaning for me. I have moved past my tragedy and found its significance. The further I have gone, the clearer it has actually become.

Each day is a one-time offer.

~Andrew E. Kaufman

Ode to Joy

One of the best parts about losing your hair from chemotherapy is the chance to get a new hairstyle or color. The wig store offers unlimited options. The place where I bought mine—aka my cranium prosthesis—had actual names for all of their products.

The wig I chose was labeled "Joy." This might seem like an oxymoron, considering my treatment for breast cancer, but I hoped it would be a prediction of things to come.

My daughter and I had great fun personifying the wig and referring to her by her name. If I walked out of the house, Joy accompanied me. She went to work, social gatherings, shopping, and church. I live in the windy panhandle of Texas, and some days it was a challenge to keep her from lifting off my head and blowing free, but she was always with me. When Joy and I came home, she went to her Styrofoam head, as I felt we both deserved a rest.

One day after work, and the appointment which concluded my second week of chemotherapy, I decided to clean my car. I went to Quick Quack, which cleans your car as you sit back and glide along. This seemed like a great idea, as my energy level was close to empty.

After the wash, I decided to vacuum the floor mats. Unfortunately, I parked a little too close to the mounted vacuum machine. I couldn't open my door but I was too tired to move the car. I figured I could squeeze into the tiny backseat and start vacuuming there. With a good deal of effort, I was able to manage that, and after wrestling with the hose to clean the front seat, I completed the job before my money ran out. However, by that time, I was exhausted and more than ready to go home. But I still had to get out of the car and return the vacuum.

The hose was still going strong, and because I was so tired, I struggled to get it out of my way and open the door. It was crowded in there, and hot, the hose was twisting over my mid-section and my patience was wearing thin. As I maneuvered myself into position to escape this predicament, I suddenly felt the desperate need to scratch my head. It was summer and Joy made me sweat. I only had one arm free to reach but I absent-mindedly lifted the vacuum up to my head. The hose instantly sucked Joy right off my bald, beautiful head. Obviously, I hadn't read the warning, explaining that the vacuum had a super duper velocity hose with enormous sucking capacity, urging all users to keep small pets and children away from it.

I wasn't surprised. I was shocked!

The darn thing wouldn't let go of Joy and my efforts to retrieve her seemed useless. She was halfway up inside the hose, stuck into the vacuum's throat, and I was struggling to reach up inside the thing and get her loose. For the first time ever, my quarters weren't running out and the vacuum kept running while both of us thrashed all over the back seat, fighting for possession of Joy.

Suddenly, I heard a very loud and hysterical laugh coming from the other side of the car. A man who had probably been watching the entire ordeal was standing next to his truck and laughing uncontrollably. When I first glanced over at him, he was holding his big belly with both hands, his face red from laughing and looking like it was going to explode. The more I struggled, the more he lost control of himself.

I am a person who normally loves to find humor in our daily lives, but in that moment I couldn't figure out exactly what was so darn funny about a bald woman wrestling with a super-sized vacuum hose, trying to retrieve the rest of her head.

As I finally excavated the last of Joy out of the vacuum, I saw that the man had tears falling from his face and he was trying to catch his breath. I very determinedly smiled and placed Joy hurriedly back upon my head, which started him all over again into convulsions of laughter.

Enough is enough, I thought. I frowned at him, and with as much dignity as possible, while trying to keep Joy in her place, I squeezed out of the small space in the back seat and got behind the driver's seat. As I glanced in the mirror, I caught a glimpse of Joy. I had inadvertently turned her upside down and that's when I lost it and started to laugh. I dumped the hose out of the back window, leaving it sprawled on the ground as I drove off, with a smile and a wave to my hysterical new friend. What a story he would have to tell his family when he got home.

As I repositioned my cranium prosthesis, I knew that my *Ode to Joy* would eventually bring smiles to others going through cancer.

~Charlotte Wheeler